To

Barbara Volk.

Thank you for your interest

I hope you find this book

useful.

Nachum Finli

Dec. 31, 1986

QUESTIONS AND ANSWERS
ABOUT TODAY'S
SECURITIES MARKET

Questions and Answers About Today's Securities Market

Nachman Bench, Ph.D.

PRENTICE-HALL, INC.
Englewood Cliffs, N.J.

Prentice-Hall International, Inc., *London*
Prentice-Hall of Australia, Pty. Ltd., *Sydney*
Prentice-Hall Canada, Inc., *Toronto*
Prentice-Hall of India Private Ltd., *New Delhi*
Prentice-Hall of Japan, Inc., *Tokyo*
Prentice-Hall of Southeast Asia Pte. Ltd., *Singapore*
Whitehall Books, Ltd., Wellington, *New Zealand*
Editora Prentice-Hall do Brasil Ltda., *Rio de Janeiro*
Prentice-Hall Hispanoamericana, S.A., *Mexico*

Library of Congress Cataloging-in-Publication Data

Bench, Nachman.
   Questions and answers about today's securities
market.

   Bibliography: p.
   Includes index.
   1. Securities. 2. Investments. I. Title.
HG4521.B429 1987   332.63′2   86-16998

ISBN 0-13-749227-8

Printed in the United States of America

DEDICATION

This book is dedicated to my wife, Adrienne, and to our children, Adam and Sarah, in appreciation for their patience and understanding that I am, again, working late to complete its writing.

How This Book Will Help You Make Money — And Keep It

Making money requires both courage and caution, but keeping it requires knowledge, intelligence, and a great deal of discipline.

A recent survey released by the New York Stock Exchange indicates that 47 million persons in the United States own shares in American businesses. That's about one fifth of the total U.S. population. This is a considerable growth from the 6.5 million persons (or 4 percent of the overall population) owning U.S. stocks and mutual funds in the early 1950s. Out of the 47 million, 22.5 are men and 22.5 are women, with children claiming the remaining 2 million.

There are winners and losers in the stock market. If you consider yourself a winner, this book will help you to preserve what you have already won. If you have lost money in the stock market, this book will help you develop a winning attitude. Most important, once you start to make money, this book will help you *keep* it.

If your objective is to make money and keep it, this book is for you. Most investors make money from time to time in the market, as most players do in the casino, but very few can keep it. The problem professional money managers and serious investors face is how to make money over a period of years and how to preserve that money.

This book will help you improve your investment performance. It is geared for the amateur and the expert alike. If you wish to preserve your capital, increase the rate of return on your investments, reduce your risk exposure, and learn how professional investment managers do it, this book is for you.

You do not need to be an expert in order to use this book, but some investment background is a plus. It's meant for someone who has made mistakes and appreciates the need of avoiding them in the future. Someone like you.

The approach in this book is basically a conservative one. You won't find any get-rich-quick schemes here. What you will find is a systematic approach that involves research and analysis for managing your money.

As you get older, your needs will change. Your need for understanding investments will grow. Whether you are planning for your retirement in a few years or in many years, you'll find this a handy reference guide for helping you accumulate funds for your own future, and for your loved ones.

You will learn how to:

- develop an investment strategy that will help you accomplish your objectives.
- hedge by using options strategies.
- use market timing indicators.
- look for undervalued stocks to reduce your downside risk and increase your upside potential.
- use technical analysis.
- reduce the risks associated with stock market investments.
- distinguish between random and nonrandom moves.

- select the right mutual fund for you.
- increase your after-tax income.
- get extra dividends per year.
- diversify your portfolio.
- use the Total Return Concept (dividends plus capital gains plus options income).
- plan for your retirement.
- select an investment advisor.
- follow a disciplined investment philosophy.
- improve communication with your brokers and the various investment experts, by becoming familiar with investment concepts.

An extensive glossary is also included to help you identify the many investment terms that you may not be familiar with.

This book is intended to be used as a reference guide. Its easy-to-read format offers straightforward answers to questions most frequently asked by investors. You can use it repeatedly, under various market conditions, as a handy source of information to help you make your investment decisions.

Cases in point are described throughout the book that give examples based on actual situations from investors. (Clients' names and other personal details have been omitted or slightly altered to protect their privacy.)

You have your own style of investing. You know what you're looking for. But you may have bad habits. This book explains some of the many risks involved and will help you pinpoint and work to change some of those habits like speculation, or the desire to get rich quick.

This book is intended to help you minimize your losses. You will learn how "not to lose." On the other hand, you will learn how to increase the rate of return on your investments without taking unnecessary risks. In short, *you* will be able to command your financial future.

Nachman Bench

Contents

CHAPTER 1

My Investment Philosophy

Like most people who invest in securities, I have made my share of mistakes. Investing is an emotional process. It requires a "disciplined approach." My philosophy is a disciplined, professional approach that evolved over many years of teaching and consulting in the field of financial analysis. It is a conservative viewpoint with a long-term perspective. You won't find any get-rich-quick schemes here. My objective has been to do better than the average, yet be consistent and preserve capital.

In 1962, while a graduate student at New York University, I received a Ford Foundation Fellowship in management science for a workshop on the use of scientific tools in financial management. This was my first exposure to the problem of decision making in finance and investment. I became a member of an investment club with some fellow students. We had all the facilities of the University's library available to us. Club members were all outstanding business students — yet every stock we bought went down. Despite the fact that we followed the textbook and did extensive research, we seemed to keep making one mistake after another. However, I was determined to learn from each mistake. I kept looking for ways to achieve better investment results.

Time passed. I graduated with a Ph.D. in 1965 and became a consultant. I spent a considerable amount of time developing computer models for stock selections and market timing indicators. During this time I interviewed many professional investors and traders to try and understand their decision-making process and criteria for consistent success.

I do not accept the idea that investing is a random process. It may not be an exact science, but it is a field of knowledge. Investing is both an art and a science. It is a process of learning and self-education. In order to be successful, you must know what you are doing. There is no substitute for experience and knowledge.

After more than 20 years of teaching and consulting in the field, I have developed my own disciplined, professional approach — my philosophy — that I will share with you now.

As an investor, you need self-discipline — to follow some fundamental rules or guidelines — if your objective is to make money and keep it. The following rules summarize my investment philosophy:

1. Preserve your capital. Don't lose it.
2. Buy stocks when their prices are low.
3. Follow the "contrarian" viewpoint.
4. Look for values — hunt for bargains.
5. Avoid unlimited risks.
6. Evaluate the potential risks versus the potential rewards.
7. Reappraise your investment holdings periodically.
8. Review the "timing" of your investment decisions.

9. Use options strategies to hedge your investments and to generate additional income.
10. Identify your investment objectives.
11. Select the portfolio that meets your investment objective.
12. Search for good information — it is eight-tenths of the battle for investment performance.
13. Learn from the past but invest in the future.
14. Beware of so-called "inside tips" that promise a quick profit.
15. Don't fall in love with a stock.
16. Evaluate the tax consequences of your investment decisions.
17. Seek professional investment advice.
18. Make sure that you end with the money, not with the dreams.
19. Don't forget the previous 18 rules.

1. PRESERVE YOUR CAPITAL. DON'T LOSE IT

Preservation of capital is one of the most important objectives of investment management. One investment mistake can wipe out the profits achieved by many other sound investments. It is relatively easy to save and accumulate financial assets. It is much more difficult to preserve them. Many who made large sums of money during their lifetimes leave estates with little or no value. You should attempt to protect as much as possible your money and assets from a decline in value.

2. BUY STOCKS WHEN THEIR PRICES ARE LOW

As an investor in the stock market, your most important concern should be the price — the price of the purchase and the price of the sale. As billionaire J. Paul Getty wrote in his book *How to Be Rich* (Chicago: Playboy Press, 1965, p.195), "Common stocks should be purchased when their prices are low, not after they have risen to high levels during an upward bull market. Buy when everyone else is selling, and hold until everyone else is buying. This is more than just a catchy slogan. It is the very essence of successful investment."

A prolonged decline in the market, when everyone is very bearish, creates an unusual buying opportunity that will probably result in substantial profits for you.

The strategy of buying stocks when the prices are low and selling stocks when prices are high involves less risk and more potential rewards than the strategy of buying high and selling higher. When prices are low, an investor buys more shares for the same amount of money than he or she does when prices are high.

Many technical advisors who are trend-followers often employ a strategy of "buy high and sell higher." They assume that the trend will continue. However, the risks involved are high because when the trend does change you may be subject to considerable losses.

CASE IN POINT: Over the years the Dow Jones Industrial Average has widely fluctuated, as the table on page 5 indicates (see also Dow Jones Industrial Average Chart on page 6).

3. FOLLOW THE "CONTRARIAN" VIEWPOINT

People think in herds. Some are desperate gamblers, others just run to the exit with the herd. Often they recover their senses slowly.

Most investors tend to follow the crowd. However, the consensus is seldom correct. What may seem obvious to most investors frequently doesn't materialize. History and experience have taught us to follow the contrarian point of view — to look for the next surprise. When everyone is optimistic (bullish), securities are usually overvalued, and that is the time when you should probably be cautious. When everyone is pessimistic (bearish), securities are usually undervalued, and that is the time when you should probably be more positive. Emotionally, it is very difficult to stand apart from the others, but this is the way to achieve superior investment performance.

Buy when everyone else is selling, and sell when everyone else is buying. Buy on market weakness, sell on strength. Don't try to buy exactly at the bottom and sell exactly at the top. You will not be able to do it. We believe that it is better to be a leader rather than a follower. Buy early and sell early. If you wait until you are "sure" that the bottom has already been reached, it may be too late to buy — you will miss the bottom. If you wait to be "sure" that the top has already been reached, it may be too late to sell — you will probably miss the top.

Dow Jones Industrial Average

Market Bottom (Time to Buy)		Market Top (Time to Sell)				%
Date	DJIA	Date		DJIA	% Change	No. of Months	Change Monthly
August 1921	64	Jan.	1926	160	+150	17	8.8
Jan. 1926	160	April	1926	140	- 13	4	3.3
April 1926	140	Sept.	1929	381	+172	41	4.2
Sept. 1929	381	July	1932	41	- 89	34	2.6
July 1932	41	March	1937	194	+373	56	6.7
March 1937	194	April	1942	93	- 52	61	0.9
April 1942	93	May	1946	212	+128	49	2.6
May 1946	212	June	1949	162	- 24	37	0.7
June 1949	162	March	1956	500	+208	81	2.6
March 1956	500	Jan.	1958	425	- 15	22	0.7
Jan. 1958	425	Jan.	1966	995	+134	96	1.4
Jan. 1966	995	May	1970	632	- 36	52	0.7
May 1970	632	Jan.	1973	1,051	+ 66	32	2.1
Jan. 1973	1,051	Dec.	1974	578	- 45	23	2.0
Dec. 1974	578	Sept.	1976	1,014	+ 44	21	2.1
Sept. 1976	1,014	Feb.	1978	750	- 26	17	1.5
Feb. 1978	750	Jan.	1981	1,005	+ 34	35	1.0
Jan. 1981	1005	June	1882	790	- 21	17	1.2
June 1982	790	Dec.	1983	1,275	+ 48	18	2.7
Dec. 1983	1275	July	1984	1,090	- 15	7	2.1
July 1984	1090	Dec.	1985	1,553	+ 42	17	2.5

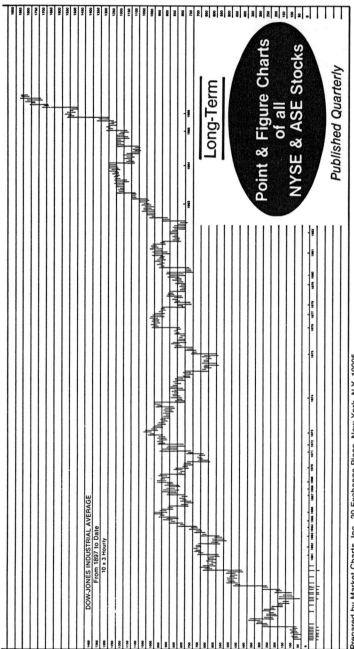

4. LOOK FOR VALUES — HUNT FOR BARGAINS

Buying stocks is similar to shopping for groceries — if you want to get the most for your money, you have to hunt for the best bargains. Careful consumers shop for bargains when they shop for their weekly groceries. It requires more time to check the labels and compare prices, but most people are willing to take that extra time in order to get the most for their money. In order to be sure that you are indeed getting a "bargain," ask yourself the following questions:

1. Is the stock selling at a fraction of the company's liquidation value?
2. Is the company worth more than the current market price of its stock?
3. Is the stock selling at a relatively low price per earning?

If you answered "yes" to these questions, chances are the stock is indeed a bargain — or at least worth a second look. But if you answered "no" to one or more of these questions, you would probably be wise to keep shopping around.

Corporate mergers, leverage buyouts, and takeovers point to the utter fallacy of that old "truth" that a stock is worth only what somebody is willing to pay for it every day in the open market.

5. AVOID UNLIMITED RISKS

Reduce the portfolio's vulnerability to big losses. One mistake can wipe out the gains achieved by many successful good investments.

Selling short a stock without the purchase of a call (an uncovered short sale) involves an unlimited degree of risk. When you sell short, you sell a stock that you do not own.

The sale of a stock when you own a call prior to exercising the call is considered a short sale. The sale of a stock when you own a warrant prior to exercising of the warrant is considered a short sale.

Selling an uncovered call (a naked call) is similar in its potential risk to selling a stock short and selling a put. When the price of a stock rises sharply, the liquidation of a short position may cost you may times the original sales price of the call. The risk is indeed very substantial. You expose yourself to an unlimited risk as the underlying stock price rises.

6. EVALUATE THE POTENTIAL RISKS VERSUS THE POTENTIAL REWARDS

Most investors, when buying a security, ask, "How much money will I make?" Yet they neglect to ask, "How much money can I lose?" It is important to compare the potential reward on your investment with the potential risk. For example, suppose you bought a stock at $30 a share. You expect the stock to increase to $40. Your potential reward is $10. If you think that the stock might decline to $26, then your potential loss is $4. Your risk/reward ratio is 10 to 4 or 2.5 to 1. When the reward/risk ratio is not favorable, you should avoid investing in that particular stock and keep your money either in a short-term bond or in a money market fund.

7. PERIODICALLY REAPPRAISE YOUR INVESTMENT HOLDINGS

Are you facing next year's market with last year's portfolio? There is nothing permanent except change. This ancienᵥ proverb still holds true. You should reappraise your investment holdings periodically because new developments may have altered their potential. Over a period of time your investment objectives may change. This in turn may require a change in your investment strategies.

You should buy a stock for several reasons. If you made a mistake and one of your assumptions did not materialize, the other reasons for the purchase may still "bail you out." If the expected takeover did not go through, the overall market may go up. If the market did not rise, the earnings may have risen.

8. REVIEW THE TIMING OF YOUR INVESTMENT DECISIONS

Accurate timing is a major factor to successful investing. Even if you buy a good stock, you could still lose money if you buy it at the wrong time. Similarly, if your timing is right, you can make money even on a speculative stock with poor corporate fundamentals. See the chapter on Market Timing Indicators.

Once the information appears on the front page of *Business Week*, it is too late to act upon. When it comes to investment decisions, what everybody knows is worthless.

9. USE OPTION STRATEGIES TO HEDGE YOUR INVESTMENTS AND TO GENERATE ADDITIONAL INCOME

The use of option writing strategies, in addition to increasing the total return of your portfolio, will help you to achieve over a number of years consistent investment returns with limited risks. See also chapter 4 "Options Hedging Strategies."

10. IDENTIFY YOUR INVESTMENT OBJECTIVES

There are various investment objectives, such as income, long-term capital appreciation, tax savings, etc. Your objectives will change as you do — depending on age, marital status, your ability to afford risk, your retirement needs, and so on. Setting realistic investment goals is the first step in selecting your appropriate investment strategy.

11. SELECT THE PORTFOLIO THAT MEETS YOUR INVESTMENT OBJECTIVES

Your choice of a particular investment strategy, and the mix of securities in your portfolio, should attempt to meet your specific, realistic investment goals. Your personal account, your retirement account, your children's account, or your corporate cash account — each one will probably have a different investment objective. Each portfolio should be managed to satisfy its unique, specific needs. For example, you may want to buy tax-free bonds for your personal account. For your retirement account, you may purchase zero coupon bonds; for your children's account, growth stocks; for your corporate account, preferred stocks to receive qualified corporate dividends.

12. SEARCH FOR GOOD INFORMATION — IT IS EIGHT-TENTHS OF THE BATTLE FOR INVESTMENT PERFORMANCE

Good information is relevant information. It can make the difference between a consistent sequence of intelligent decisions and "shot in the dark" random decisions. The other two-tenths of the battle for investment performance depends on using the appropriate investment strategy.

13. LEARN FROM THE PAST BUT INVEST IN THE FUTURE

Experience is the best teacher. Historical statistical information should be used to understand both market behavior and the company's past performance. On the other hand, old information that is known to everyone has little value. When making investment decisions, future earnings are much more important than past earnings. For example, a company that lost money last year to the point of near-bankruptcy, could turn around next year and find itself with a very promising and profitable future. The stock in this case would go up despite its poor past performance. One such example is the Chrysler Corporation. It was near bankruptcy in 1980, yet the price of its stock rose from $3.50 in 1981 to $35 in 1983 — a tenfold increase.

14. BEWARE OF SO-CALLED "INSIDE TIPS" THAT PROMISE A QUICK PROFIT

Don't listen to tips from "barbers and beauticians" on how to get rich quickly. You don't get something for nothing. Accumulating wealth is a slow process. It requires knowledge and patience.

CASE IN POINT: Mr. R. T. called me with a tip from his Washington friend. He expected one of the military defense contracting companies to be awarded a large contract. He purchased some short-term calls at $2 a call with the prospective contracting company. One week later an announcement was made that the contract had been awarded to another company. The common stock took a slide and so did the call option. Mr. R. T. wanted a quick profit — he ended up with a quick loss.

Mr. R. T. was of course very disappointed. He decided to wait until the future earnings of the company improved or to see if the company is awarded another contract. However, a call option has an expiration date. After that date, it has no value. Waiting for positive future developments will not benefit the owner of the option. If Mr. R. T. had bought the common stock of the prospective company, waiting for better future developments, he could have prevented a capital loss.

15. DON'T FALL IN LOVE WITH A STOCK

Very often an investor will "fall in love" with a stock. It may be in a glamorous field such as computers or space exploration. You should always remember that the final test is return on investment, and this requires a cool, continuous appraisal of the stock. Avoid the emotional attachment you may have toward a particular company.

CASE IN POINT: Ten years ago, Mrs. O. received as a gift from her parents 500 shares of the common stock of American Telephone and Telegraph (AT&T). For over a century, this had been known as the stock of "widows and orphans." Ma Bell had been one of the most regulated companies. It was big, safe, and probably owned by more shareholders than any other company.

Recently Mrs. O. came to me and asked me to manage her portfolio. We discussed her investment objectives and determined that she needed income and safety for her pending retirement. After reviewing her portfolio, she told me that I would have discretionary trading authority to buy and sell whatever I thought appropriate. However, I was not to sell her AT&T stock! Obviously she was in love with the stock for sentimental reasons.

In 1982, AT&T accepted the Justice Department's proposal for a modified consent decree that required a drastic restructuring of the Bell System. AT&T, which had until this time been a powerful monopoly, was reorganized into a new AT&T and seven regional companies. The seven regional companies are: Ameritech, Bell Atlantic, Bell South, Nynex, Pacific Telesis, Southwestern Bell, and U.S. West.

The new AT&T is no longer the safe widow's and orphan's stock. After the divestiture, the company offers a lower dividend yield and a greater degree of uncertainty of future earnings. It is a more volatile stock. As a technological company, it faces tough competition from IBM, MCI, and GTE.

Mrs. O's decision to keep her AT&T stock was based on sentimental reasons. It was not based on the current outlook for earnings and dividends. The company has gone through a major reorganization and no longer fits Mrs. O's investment objectives and needs. Companies change with time. A periodic review is necessary to determine if the stock should be held or sold.

It was a mistake on Mrs. O's part to instruct me to hold on to her AT&T stock, regardless of any new developments. She should have been willing to look at AT&T in the same way as she would any other stock.

16. EVALUATE THE TAX CONSEQUENCES OF YOUR INVESTMENT DECISIONS

You should compare the return available from tax-free securities with the return available from taxable securities. Consult your tax advisor periodically to keep abreast of any changes in the tax laws. Future changes in federal, state, and local taxes may necessitate an adjustment in your investment strategy.

17. SEEK PROFESSIONAL ADVICE

You may be an expert in your professional field — a highly qualified lawyer, accountant, or medical doctor — but that doesn't mean you know how to invest your own money. You may be a business executive specializing in advertising, marketing, or production, but not necessarily in business investments. The field of investments is a specialized area which requires a considerable amount of training and concentration. For this reason, you should consult on an ongoing basis with investment professionals.

18. MAKE SURE THAT YOU END WITH THE MONEY, NOT WITH THE DREAMS

On Wall Street some investors begin with dreams and end up with the money; others begin with the money and end up with the dreams. If you follow the guidelines presented here, the odds are in your favor that you will end with the money, and not with the dreams.

Successful investment begins with knowledge. Knowledge begins and ends in experience, but it does not end in the experience in which it begins.

Set realistic goals, and then plan and execute an investment strategy to help you attain these objectives.

19. DON'T FORGET THE PREVIOUS 18 RULES

Making money requires both courage and caution, but keeping it requires knowledge, intelligence, and a great deal of discipline.

Rule 19 is this: Don't forget the previous 18 rules.

CHAPTER 2

Investment Risks: 14 Important Factors to Consider

When most investors purchase securities, they look at the upside potential — that is, how much money will they make? Only a few look at the downside potential — namely, how much money can they lose? Investment risks are the degree of uncertainty in capital appreciation and income from investments in the future. Investment results cannot be guaranteed. There is no escaping it — every investment alternative involves some degree of risk. The following is a list of the 14 most common risks investors may encounter:

Competition
Corporate Earnings
Economic Cycle
Industry-Wide Problems

Inflation
Interest Rates
Market Liquidity
Market Timing
Top Management Personnel
Government Regulation
Foreign Countries
Overconcentration in Few Investments
Lawsuits and Consumer Claims
Changes in the Tax Laws

The investment strategy you choose should be structured to protect your investments from the various risks. Do not overexpose your portfolio to one particular risk.

COMPETITION RISK

By the very nature of the American economic system, every business is subject to some degree of competition. For example, suppose you are in the market for a new car. You have literally dozens of domestic and foreign models from which to choose — in a variety of styles and price ranges suited to your individual needs and preferences. In the pharmaceutical industry, a company may develop a new drug that could make a competing company's product obsolete. In the field of high technology, products can become obsolete within a matter of years or months. As an investor, you should always be alert to changes in leadership of various competing companies.

Foreign competition has been another major risk to U.S. corporations.

CASE IN POINT: Texas Instruments (listed on the New York Stock Exchange under the symbol TXN) has been known for many years as a high-quality technology growth stock. During the early 1970s, it sold for an average of over 30 times price per earnings. In 1983 the stock reached $175 a share. In 1984, the company's semiconductor business segment generated over half a billion dollars in operating profits. Low demand and industrywide overcapacity sparked fierce price competition. In 1985, the same segment of the business lost money, dropping to $86 a share. The semiconductor boom slumped drastically, due basically to competition from Japanese companies.

CASE IN POINT: In 1981, the Wheeling-Pittsburgh steel corporation (one of the 10 largest steel producers in the United States) was selling at $40 a share. In 1985, the company underwent reorganization proceedings pursuant to Chapter 11 of the Federal Bankruptcy Code, and its common stock declined to $7 — a victim to foreign imports. Similarly, LTV Corp., the second largest steel producer in the United States in 1985, watched its stock decline from $24 in 1981 to $6 in 1985. LTV's merger with Republic Steel, which was designed to generate increased earnings, actually led to larger losses. Only its aerospace and defense business kept it from bankruptcy.

CORPORATE EARNINGS RISK

Corporate earnings can fluctuate considerably from month to month and year to year. The value of every investment is related to the company's earnings outlook. A deterioration in earnings or earnings outlook could result in a substantial decline in the price of any stock.

CASE IN POINT: In 1981, oil field services stocks did very well on the stock market, when the demand for drilling was at its peak. As oil prices declined, the demand for these drilling services rapidly diminished. The earnings of the companies in the industry rapidly deteriorated as did the price of the stocks. For example, Smith International was selling near $60 a share in 1981, and dropped to $8 a share by 1985. Its earnings dropped from a high of $5.80 in 1981 to a deficit of $3.01 in 1984. Reading and Bates sold for $32 in 1981, and was down to $6 in 1985. Its earnings dropped from a high of $3.01 in 1981 to a deficit of $1.60 in 1985.

Past earnings performance is not a guarantee for future results. The price of a stock is related not only to last year's earnings, but also to the trend of earnings. Often, the price per earning ratio depends on the historical trend of earning growth.

ECONOMIC CYCLE RISK

The sales and earnings of many industries (steel, automobile, chemical, building, etc.) will change depending on changes in the economic cycle. During a business recession (a slowdown in economic activity), the sales and earnings of cyclical companies will decline. As an investor, you should not get overconfident at the peak of the cycle, or unduly pessimistic at the bottom of the cycle.

CASE IN POINT: General Motors' (GM) business is cyclical in nature. As a result, the price of GM stock has fluctuated sharply according to the economic cycles. In 1962, GM stock sold for $45 a share. By 1965, the price had reached $110 per share. In 1970, it had dropped back to $60. In 1971, it rose to $90. During the 1975 economic recession, the price dropped to a low of $30. In the economic recovery of 1976, the stock rose back up to $75, then dropped back down to $35 during the 1981-1982 recession. During the 1984-85 economic recovery, the stock rose from $35 to $85.

INDUSTRY-WIDE PROBLEMS RISK

A specific industry may have unique problems at one period or another. For example, when the price of oil rises, all the airlines are adversely affected. Similarly, when mortgage rates go up, building stocks suffer. When the dollar is strong on the foreign exchange, the earnings of U.S. companies with large foreign sales decline.

CASE IN POINT: The airline industry was booming in the late 1960s. Yet by 1974-1975, it was in a major slump. The slump (due to the increase in the price of oil) was felt throughout the industry and was not limited to one particular airline. The following table shows the drastic decline in the price of several airlines' shares:

Airline	Price per Share	
	1967	1975
Eastern	$60	$ 5
KLM	$30	$ 3
Pan American	$35	$ 3
UAL	$85	$15

INFLATION RISK

Inflation can be defined as rising prices and costs of goods and services (food, rent, wages, etc.). In effect, for the same quantity and quality of goods and services, you have to pay more than previously. Inflation is hard on everyone, especially on retired persons and those who may have invested heavily in long-term bonds. Let's look at these two areas more closely.

Inflation hurts most retired people because they often must depend on fixed retirement income. As prices go up, you, as a retired person, may have to spend more money to maintain the same standard of living, while at the same time your income may remain unchanged.

In many cases, because of improper financial planning, retired people have to reduce their standard of living. Namely, they can afford to buy fewer goods and services.

When you buy fixed income bonds maturing in the year 2010, you are subject to the risk of inflation. As interest rates rise bond values decline. You may be locked into a 12 percent interest return when the available return from alternative investments may be 15 percent. You do not keep up with inflation.

You must hedge against inflation. Buy assets (such as real estate) with borrowed funds. Inflation favors the borrower at the expense of the creditor. Government spending of unearned money is the root of inflation. Future inflation rate is likely to be worse during the next 10 to 20 years than it has been over the past decade.

Real estate over the long term may be a good hedge against inflation (especially if purchased with a low-interest mortgage). Similarly, common stocks, over a long period of time, also have proven to be a good hedge against inflation.

Buy securities that will benefit from inflation; for example, gold and silver stocks. You must make more money and increase your return on investment to protect from the risk of inflation.

Chart 1
LONG-TERM INTEREST RATES 1800-1977

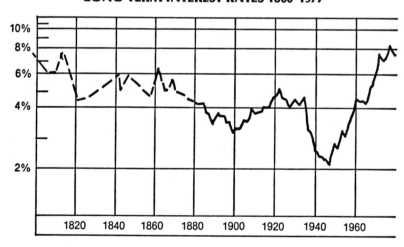

INTEREST RATE RISK

Interest rates can go up or down yearly due to changes in Federal reserve monetary policy, the rate of inflation, and the demand for capital. As shown in Chart 1, from 1800 to 1870 the yield on long-term U.S. government bonds fluctuated between a high of about 8 percent to a low of about 4.5 percent. Prime corporate bonds have had high volatility in yield from 1880 to date. In 1920, the yield rose to about 5 percent and then declined to about 2¼ percent in the early 1940s. Rates rose steadily from the early 1940s to 1977, when they reached the 8 percent level (first reached in 1800).

Chart 2
U.S. TREASURIES 30 YEARS 1977-1985

Chart 2 shows how the yield on long-term U.S. Treasuries rose from about 7¾ percent in 1977 to 15 percent in 1981. It then declined to 10.5 percent in 1982 and rose to about 13.5 percent in 1984. It dropped to 10 percent in 1985.

The federal funds rate (the negotiated interest rate charged by one bank when it loans excessive reserves to another bank that needs to increase its reserve) is the most sensitive indicator of monetary conditions. Chart 3 indicates the wide fluctuations in that rate from 1974 to 1985.

In 1976, the rate was near 5 percent when the Federal Reserve policy was accommodative. It rose sharply to 20 percent in 1981, when the Federal Reserve policy became very restrictive.

Chart 3
FEDERAL FUNDS RATE 1974-1985

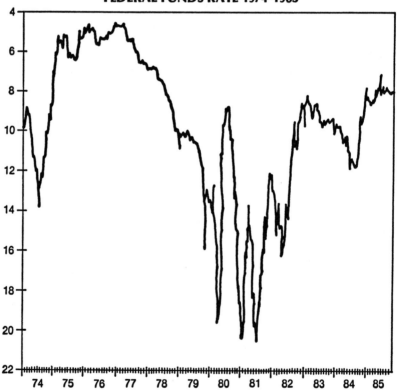

Stock prices, in many cases, will fluctuate in direct correlation with interest rate. When interest rates go down, stock prices usually rise as the dividend yield from common stock becomes relatively attractive. As interest rates go up, stocks usually decline (negative correlation) because investment in bonds becomes more attractive.

CASE IN POINT: In 1963 the yield on long-term corporate Aaa bonds was about 4.2 percent. The yield steadily rose from 1963 to 1974 when it reached a peak of 9.2 percent. During the same period, the Dow Jones Utilities Average declined from a peak of 163 in 1963 to a low of 75 in 1974 (a loss of 88 points or 54 percent of investment value). Stocks of regulated utilities are sensitive to fluctuations in interest rates. They have been considered a relatively safe income-producing investment. However, they are subject to interest rate risk. When interest rates go up, utility stocks decline; when interest rates decline, utility stocks appreciate in value.

MARKET LIQUIDITY RISK

Although the U.S. security market (New York Stock Exchange, American Stock Exchange, Over the Counter) is the largest and most liquid in the world, under certain market conditions or in the case of smaller companies, you may have difficulty selling a large number of shares. If you had to sell your stock in a hurry, your investment return could suffer simply because you might be forced to sell at a lower price due to lack of liquidity in the marketplace. Higher future levels of interest rate is a major risk to long-term securities investments.

MARKET TIMING RISK

The value of your investment could decline due to a market decline, with no relationship to the performance of the company. (See the chapter on Market Timing.)

In October 1929 the Dow Jones Industrial Average reached a peak of 381.17. Within three years this Dow average dropped to 41.12. It was a drop of 339.95 points or 89 percent.

In January 1973 the Dow Jones Industrial Average reached 1051.70. Within two years, by December 1974, it dropped to 577.60 — a drop of 474.10 points or 45 percent.

In January 1984 the Dow Jones Industrial Average reached 1296. Six months later, in July, it dropped to 1079 — a drop of 217 points or 16.7 percent.

TOP MANAGEMENT PERSONNEL RISK

The performance of many companies is directly related to the ability of top management. When a top executive resigns or is hired by a competitor, the company will suffer and so will its stock.

GOVERNMENT REGULATION RISK

Many industries are subject to government regulation and intervention. For example, in the drug industry the Food and Drug Administration (FDA) may prohibit a company from marketing a new product or force it to discontinue a previously successful product because of possible adverse health effects. Nuclear power plants have swung from one extreme to another during the past decade. What may be hailed as the "technology of the future" could be denounced as a potential health hazard a few years later.

> CASE IN POINT: The stock of Long Island Lighting dropped from $16 a share in 1983 to $5 a share in 1984 because the Federal Nuclear Regulatory Commission would not approve a full-power testing of its Shoreham nuclear plant until an emergency evacuation plan was in place.

Moreover, the governor of New York State, Mario Cuomo, was opposed to the plant's operation. This was a clear case of the risk of government regulations in a regulated industry.

FOREIGN COUNTRIES

The sales and profits of many companies come from foreign businesses. Revolutions, unstable governments, and fluctuating economies in the foreign nations can significantly alter a company's anticipated revenues. For this reason, a dollar earned abroad does not have the same value as a dollar earned in the United States. A company's assets in foreign countries should be discounted to reflect the above risks.

Investments in foreign countries and foreign securities involves a higher degree of risk than investing in U.S. companies and securities.

CASE IN POINT: ASA (a closed-end investment company) traded at about $80 a share in 1983. The value of ASA shares is directly influenced by the value of South African mining shares. In September of 1985 ASA shares dropped to $35 a share. The U.S. government has no direct control over the South African government's policies, which indirectly influence the value of ASA's shares.

OVERCONCENTRATION IN A FEW INVESTMENTS

Investors in some cases tend to "fall in love with" and overconcentrate their investment in a particular stock. This could involve a high degree of risk. Fortunes of companies do change, and what may seem to be an excellent company with a promising future today could end up bankrupt due to technological innovations in just a few years.

LAWSUITS AND CONSUMER CLAIMS

More and more companies are subject to lawsuits and claims by consumers. These lawsuits could be very damaging to the company's financial well-being as well as the shareholders'. Drug companies and other corporations dealing with health-related products are especially vulnerable to this kind of risk.

CASE IN POINT: Manville Corporation, a leading producer of insulations, sold at $32 a share in 1980. By 1982 the price of its shares dropped to $5 per share, the subject of major asbestos-related lawsuits and consumer claims. As a result, it declared bankruptcy under chapter 11.

CASE IN POINT: A.H. Robins Co., a manufacturer of ethical pharmaceuticals, established a 1984 year-end reserve of $650 million to cover damage health claims by consumers who used the Dalkon Shield birth control product. As of 1985, Robins was a defendant in nearly 4,500 lawsuits, with most of the lawsuits claiming both compensatory and punitive damages for alleged serious physical injury caused by the formerly sold intrauterine contraceptive device. The stock, which had reached $24 per share in 1983, dropped to $10 in 1985.

CHANGES IN THE TAX LAW

Tax laws are subject to frequent changes. Investors invest assuming that the current tax advantages will continue in the future. However, as tax laws and tax rates change, the advantages and disadvantages of various investment alternatives will also change. For example, the income from a tax-free bond may no longer be tax-free. The maximum tax rate on individual tax rate might change from 50 percent to 30 percent. The advantage in a tax-sheltered investment may disappear because of updated tax laws.

CONCLUSION

Understanding the various risks associated with investments in the various securities markets will help you avoid their potentially adverse financial consequences. You will also enjoy a new peace of mind.

How much risk should I assume?

The level of risk you should take depends on your age, personality, financial situation, plans for retirement, and living expenses needs. Try to minimize the risks involved without sacrificing potential returns.

Gold is considered a safe investment, but at $800 at the beginning of 1980 it was a very risky investment (and so was silver at $45).

Future developments that may affect stock market prices are difficult to predict. For example, an executive or president of a company may suddenly die. It is not always possible to foresee the various developments that may reduce or increase the risks involved. However, it is necessary for you as an investor to continuously evaluate each risk and compare one to another. This will help you determine the potential rewards versus the potential risks when making investment decisions. The more experience you have in the investment field, the more you become aware of the risks involved.

Most amateur investors are simply not aware of the risks or the potential of losing money. Evaluating the various risks, comparing them to each other, and deciding how much risk to assume is not an exact science. It is a matter of personal judgment and the willingness and monetary ability to take risks. For example, a wealthy individual, with a portfolio of $2 million, can afford to take risks that an investor with a $100,000 portfolio cannot.

A statistician may define risk as "equal to expected loss"; i.e.,

$$\text{risk} = \text{a month at risk} \times \text{probability of loss}$$

It is difficult to use this definition in the practical, uncertain world of investment.

There are two general kinds of risks: (1) not knowing everything about a present condition (this is a statistical uncertainty), and (2) being unable to predict the future condition. Some investors are "risk lovers"; they actually seek risky investments. Other investors are "risk avoiders"; they prefer to limit their risks to the smallest amount possible.

Whenever investment decisions are made on the basis of incomplete information, there are risks of making an incorrect decision — a decision that would not have been made if complete information had been available.

CHAPTER 3

Investment Concepts and Strategies

INVESTMENT ALTERNATIVES

The securities market covers many different, individual, and separate markets: the stock market, bond market, commodity market, low-priced issues market, international markets, government bonds, municipal bonds, real estate, precious metals, and so on. Each market has its own characteristics that may appeal to a different group of investors depending on their needs at that particular time.

What investment alternatives are available to me?

The following are some investment alternatives you may wish to consider depending on your specific circumstances and overall market and economic condition:

Cash
Money market funds
Certificates of deposit (CDs)
Treasury securities
Common stock
Common stock, plus option writing strategies
Various options strategies
Corporate bonds
Municipal bonds
Municipal trusts
Convertible bonds
Precious metals (gold, silver)
Foreign securities
Collectibles: stamps, coins, art
Real estate
Diamonds
Tax shelters
Mutual funds
Commodities

How can I select from among all the available investment alternatives?

The selection of your best investment alternative depends on several factors. In addition to your unique personal needs, you should review the following:

1. Outlook for the economy
2. Future rate of inflation
3. Interest rate trends
4. Value of the dollar relative to other foreign currencies
5. Federal budget deficits
6. New tax regulations
7. Stock market trends
8. Bond market trends
9. Potential risks and potential rewards associated with each investment alternative

CASH

Like a general who doesn't keep his troops fighting all the time, an investor should not always be fully invested. There are times when stock and bond prices are too high, and in order to preserve your capital, you should be "out of the market." Although cash does not earn any interest, there are times when it is prudent to temporarily "park" your money until a better alternative develops. For example, during periods when the stock market goes down, most stocks will also decline. When interest rates rise, bond prices decline. Selling your stocks and bonds at such times and keeping the funds in cash will protect you from losses. Since cash does not produce any income, money should not be kept as cash for any long periods of time. Instead, it should be moved to a money market fund.

MONEY MARKET FUNDS

The objective of money market funds is to pay a high current income to the extent consistent with the preservation of capital. Money market funds achieve this objective by investing only in money market obligations with maturities of one year or less, including bank certificates of deposit, bankers' acceptances, high-grade commercial paper, and securities issued or guaranteed by the United States government or its agencies and instrumentalities.

Money market funds are no-load, diversified, open-end management investment companies.

As an investor in a money market fund, you may request a supply of checks. You can use these money market checks as you would use any ordinary commercial bank checks, except that money market checks may not be certified and usually cannot be written for less than $250. When you use a check to make a redemption, it enables you as a shareholder in the fund to receive daily dividends on the shares to be redeemed up to and including the business day the checks cleared. Usually there is no charge to shareholders for this checking service. Most money market funds accept telephone requests for redemption from shareholders who elect this option. The proceeds of such a redemption can be sent only to the shareholder at his or her address or bank account.

Money market funds pay dividends equal to the entire net investment income including realized gains and losses, if any, on each business day. Funds declare dividends for Saturdays, Sundays, and holidays on the previous fund business day. All dividends and distributions of capital gains are automatically invested in additional shares of the fund immediately upon payment. Dividends declared by money market funds are taxable to shareholders as ordinary income, notwithstanding that all dividends and distributions are reinvested in additional shares.

Tax-free money market funds provide investors with high current interest income exempt from income taxes. This objective is achieved by investing primarily in short-term, high quality, tax-exempt obligations issued by state and municipal governments and by public authorities. These funds seek to maintain a constant net asset value of $1.00 per share.

BONDS

A bond is a debt obligation or a liability of a borrower. When you buy a bond, in effect, you are lending money that will be repaid on the bond's maturity date. Many bonds are traded in the various bond markets (New York Stock Exchange, American Stock Exchange, Over the Counter). You can sell your bond prior to maturity at current market prices, which may be lower, the same, or higher than the face value of the bond.

Interest payment on a bond is an obligation of the borrower, unlike corporate cash or stock dividends, which are declared by the board of directors and are not an obligation of the corporation.

Bond Ratings

How do I determine the safety of a bond?

Most bonds are rated by Moody's Investors Service and Standard & Poor's Corp. The ratings assigned are a reflection of the safety of the bonds. The following is an explanation of the various corporate bond ratings, as published by the rating services:

Moody's Investors Service, Inc.

Aaa. Bonds which are rated Aaa are judged to be of the best quality. They carry the smallest degree of investment risk and are generally referred to as "gilt-edge." Interest payments are protected by a large or by an exceptionally stable margin and principal is secure. While the various protective elements are likely to change, such changes as can be visualized are most unlikely to impair the fundamentally strong position of such issues.

Aa. Bonds which are rated Aa are judged to be of high quality by all standards. Together with the Aaa group they comprise what are generally known as high grade bonds. They are rated lower than the best bonds because margins of protection may not be as large as in Aaa securities, fluctuation of protective elements may be of greater amplitude or there may be other elements present which make the long-term risks appear somewhat larger than in Aaa securities.

A. Bonds which are rated A possess many favorable investment attributes and are considered as upper-medium grade obligations. Factors giving security to principal and interest are considered adequate but elements may be present which suggest a susceptibility to impairment sometime in the future.

Baa. Bonds which are rated Baa are considered as medium grade obligations; i.e., they are neither highly protected nor poorly secured. Interest payments and principal security appear adequate for the present but certain protective elements may be lacking or may be character-istically unreliable over any great length of time. Such bonds lack outstanding investment characteristics and in fact have speculative characteristics as well.

     Ba. Bonds which are rated Ba are judged to have speculative elements; their future cannot be considered well-assured. Often the protection of interest and principal payments may be very moderate and thereby not well safeguarded during both good and bad times over the future. Uncertainty of position characterizes bonds in this class.

     B. Bonds rated B generally lack characteristics of the desirable investment. Assurance of interest and prin-cipal payments or of maintenance of other terms of the contract over any long period of time may be small.

     Caa. Bonds which are rated Caa are of poor stand-ing. Such issues may be in default or there may be present elements of danger with respect to principal or interest.

     Ca. Bonds which are rated Ca represent obligations which are speculative in a high degree. Such issues are often in default or have other marked shortcomings.

Standard & Poor's Corporation

     AAA. This is the highest rating assigned by Stand-ard & Poor's to a debt obligation and indicates an extreme-ly strong capacity to pay principal and interest.

     AA. Bonds rated AA also qualify as high-quality debt obligations. Capacity to pay principal and interest is very strong, and in the majority of instances they differ from AAA issues only in small degree.

     A. Bonds rated A have a strong capacity to pay principal and interest, although they are somewhat more susceptible to the adverse effects of changes in circum-stances and economic conditions.

     BBB. Bonds rated BBB are regarded as having an adequate capacity to pay principal and interest. Whereas they normally exhibit protection parameters, adverse economic conditions or changing circumstances are more likely to lead to a weakened capacity to pay principal and interest for bonds in this capacity than for bonds in the A category.

BB, B, CCC, CC. Bonds rated BB, B, CCC, and CC are regarded, on balance, as predominantly speculative with respect to the issuer's capacity to pay interest and repay principal in accordance with the terms of the obligations. BB indicates the lowest degree of speculation and CC the highest degree of speculation. While such bonds will likely have some quality and protective characteristics, these are outweighed by large uncertainties or major risk exposures to adverse conditions.

C. The rating C is reserved for income bonds on which no interest is currently being paid.

D. Debt rated D is in default, and payment of interest and/or repayment of principal is in arrears.

NR. Indicates that no rating has been requested, that there is insufficient information on which to base a rating, or that S&P does not rate a particular type of obligation as a matter of policy.

CONVERTIBLE BONDS

A convertible bond has the following characteristics:

1. First, it is a bond. It has all the characteristics (including relative safety) of a regular bond.
2. It is convertible, which gives its holder the right to exchange it (at predetermined stated terms — prices and periods) for common stock in the underlying company.

What are the advantages of convertible bonds?

Investors like the appreciation potential offered by common stocks, but many must forego these equity investments because of the risk associated with their price volatility.

The value of convertible bonds usually rises and falls in value with the common stock. Most convertibles have a higher current income return than the underlying common stocks. Their income is more secure than the common stock dividend. (A common stock dividend can be cut, postponed, or eliminated.)

Investing in convertible bonds is a way to have your cake and eat it too. Bonds convertible into common stock let you participate in the upside potential should the company do well. On the other hand, should the price of the stock go down or remain unchanged, the convertible bond remains a bond and therefore has less downside risk. You have both the security of a bond and the potential appreciation of a stock.

What are the disadvantages of a convertible bond?

Not all convertibles will always be favorably priced. A convertible bond could be overpriced relative to the underlying common stock. The total return (income plus capital appreciation) could be less than the total return from the common stock. It is not advantageous to buy a convertible bond under such conditions.

Once I convert the convertible bond into the common stock can I reverse the action and reconvert the stock into the bond?

No. Once the bond has been converted into a stock, you cannot reconvert it into the bond.

DISCOUNT BONDS

Due to market conditions, from time to time bonds may sell at a discount from face value.

What are the advantages of buying discount bonds on margin?

Leveraging these bonds through margin purchases can greatly enhance after-tax yields. You capitalize on the fact that ordinary tax deductions may be obtained for net borrowing costs, while the market discount is eligible for capital gain treatment.

What are "baby bonds"?

Regular bonds usually have a face value of $1,000. Baby bonds usually have a face value of $100.

U.S. GOVERNMENT SECURITIES

The market for U.S. government securities is by far the largest, most active, and most liquid market in the world. They are one of the safest investments available today because the U.S. government agrees to pay these debt obligations at maturity.

Which marketable U.S. government securities can I buy in the open marketplace?

The term "U.S. government securities" covers a variety of investments. You can invest in securities directly issued by the U.S. government such as Treasury bills, Treasury notes, and Treasury bonds. Treasury bills mature in less than one year. Treasury notes mature between one and 10 years. Treasury bonds mature between five and 35 years. Treasury bills are issued at a discount from face value.

You can also invest in federal agencies' securities, which are guaranteed by the full faith and credit of the U.S. government. These include: Federal National Mortgage Association, Federal Farm Credit, Federal Home Loan, Federal Intermediate Credit, Federal Land Bank, and GNMA issues.

GNMA INVESTING

What are GNMAs, and what advantages or disadvantages are there in investing in them?

The Government National Mortgage Association (GNMA) buys home mortgages from lending banks and guarantees them by making them the collateral for GNMA certificates. These certificates are bought by individual investors who own a portion of a diversified portfolio of mortgages.

These GNMA certificates are attractive because they are relatively safe and often offer a higher interest rate return than regular Treasury securities. Investors also receive monthly interest payments. These payments consist of both interest and principal.

The disadvantage of owning a GNMA is that when the overall level of interest rates declines, the borrower is inclined to prepay the existing mortgages with its relatively high rates. For that reason, an investor in GNMAs could experience an earlier than expected redemption and may have to reinvest the proceeds at a lower rate of return.

MUNICIPAL BONDS

These are debts securities that are issued by a state or a city or a political subdivision. They are exempt from all federal taxes. For that reason, they are attractive to individual investors who are in a high tax bracket.

What are the objectives of municipal bond swaps?

In a municipal bond swap, you sell your bonds to realize losses and reinvest the proceeds in different, higher coupon-yielding securities. This is done to achieve two objectives:

1. Your realized losses can shelter realized gains, particularly short-term capital gains.

2. The proceeds can be reinvested in different municipal bonds, with higher coupon yields to produce additional tax-free income. With today's high level of interest rates and the depressed prices of old bonds, swaps can be particularly attractive to certain investors.

MUNICIPAL SECURITIES TRUSTS

A municipal securities trust is a unit investment trust, usually organized by an investment firm, that selects a specific number (10 to 50) of tax-exempt bonds. Units of the trust are sold to investors with a minimum investment of usually $5,000.

What are the unique features of municipal securities trusts?

1. **High current tax-exempt income.**
   You can choose from among monthly, semi-annual, or annual income payments.

2. **Diversification.**
   The trust's portfolio is usually invested in 10 to 50 different bonds and in several states; however, specific state trusts will invest only in the states specified in the prospectus. For example, a New York trust will invest only in New York bonds to satisfy the tax-advantage needs of New York state residents.

3. **Specific minimum investment grade rating (for example, A or better as rated by Standard & Poor's).**
   If every municipal bond in the trust is rated A or better, you enjoy a relatively low-risk investment.

4. **Known fixed maturity dates.**
   Trusts are quoted on an average life basis. For example, some of the bonds in the trust may mature in 29 years, some in 30, and some in 31 years — the average life would be 30 years. As the bonds in the trust mature, the owner of the units of the trust will be paid out until the trust is liquidated.

5. **Easy resale.**
   You have instant liquidity at current market value. Investment firms usually make a market in the trusts they organized.

6. **Convenience.**
   Unit holders do not have to monitor or evaluate the portfolio for calls, refundings, or bonds coming to

maturity. The professionals who supervise the trust will do it for you. In addition, the trustee safekeeps the trust's bonds, clips coupons, and collects interest. You also get one check monthly, semi-annually, or annually, at your preference.

7. **Professional management.**
   A diversified portfolio of municipal bonds is selected by municipal professionals to give you high current tax-exempt income.

8. **Management and redemption fees.**
   Most trusts do not charge management or redemption fees.

9. **Tax swap opportunities.**
   Timely maneuvers during the year can help you gain a tax-favored position. The prudent use of the trusts' units in swapping may let you consolidate portions of your portfolio, possibly increase current income, or lessen taxes without losing current income or par value of holdings.

10. **Preservation of yield.**
    Should interest rates decline in the future, you will not suffer a decline in your income. You will earn current rates, at compounded interest, as long as you own the units.

11. **Reinvestment plans**
    Unit holders usually have the choice to reinvest interest income in units of available series of municipal trusts.

MUNICIPAL SECURITIES TRUSTS — DISCOUNT SERIES

The discount series uses zero-coupon bonds and discount bonds to give you both substantial tax-free capital appreciation that will enable you to substantially increase your investment at maturity and current high tax-exempt income.

Municipal Securities Trusts discount series are made up of both municipal revenue interest-bearing bonds and zero-coupon bonds. Zero-coupon bonds pay no interest now but deliver substantial appreciation at maturity, tax-free.

ZERO-COUPON OBLIGATIONS

What are the advantages of zero-coupon obligations?

Zero-coupon obligations are purchased at substantial discount from their face value. They do not pay any current income interest. For that reason, they are very convenient. You do not have to be concerned with the reinvesting of interest payments, as in the case of a regular bond.

As a holder of a zero-coupon obligation, you will receive the full face value at maturity. When you purchase the bond, you know exactly what your return is.

The longer the maturities, the lower the price you will pay for the zero coupon obligation, which enables you to purchase more bonds. For example, suppose you want to give your grandchild, who is three years old, a $10,000 gift at the time he will enter college. Assuming a yield to maturity of 11.6 percent, you can buy today for about $1,700 a zero-coupon bond with a face value of $10,000 maturing in 15 years.

CATS (Certificates of Accrual on Treasury Securities)

As an investor in CATS, you buy zero-coupon U.S. Treasury obligations. The reasons for their popularity include:

1. Since they are direct obligations of the U.S. government, they are a low-risk investment.
2. There are a variety of maturities from which to choose. Over 50 maturities are available, ranging from less than one year to more than 20 years in maturity.
3. There is an active secondary market, which provides trading liquidity.

4. Yield to maturity is guaranteed because there are no coupon payments and no reinvestment risks.

5. CATS are available in small denominations beginning at $1,000 face value. If you buy CATS at 50 percent discount, you will pay $500 for a $1,000 face certificate.

CATS are ideal investments for IRA and Keogh accounts, as well as corporate pension and profit sharing plans, and for nonprofit organizations.

PREFERRED STOCKS

Preferred stocks have the following characteristics:

1. A stated rule of dividends, often with cumulative dividends rights. In the case of a cumulative preferred stock, if the company does not pay the stated dividend in any year, the company will have to pay the cumulative dividends for each year that it did not pay previously (current plus any arrears).

2. A priority to any payment of dividends on the common stock. Full preferred dividends are mandatory if the common shareholders receive any dividends.

3. The right, in the event of liquidation, to receive payments before any are made to the common shareholders.

Preferred stocks sometimes are callable by the company at a specific price. (The company has the right to purchase the stock from you at the stated price.) You should determine the details of the call feature before you invest in any preferred stock.

DIVERSIFICATION

Many investors fail to consider the risks of concentrating their investments in one company or in one industry. It is a common mistake, as many investors "fall in love" with a particular stock. Diversification helps you to spread the risks and reduce your exposure to one mistake.

CASE IN POINT: In the early 1980s, Mrs. T. found herself a widow at the age of 60. Her husband left an estate worth over $1 million at the time of his death. There were only two securities in the portfolio, and both were in the same industry of oil drilling. This portfolio obviously was overconcentrated. If the portfolio had been left unchanged, its value would have declined by 50 percent within a period of two years, due to the sharp price decline in oil drilling stocks. Furthermore, the two stocks paid very little dividend, yet Mrs. T. needed income from the portfolio for living expenses.

My recommendation, as an investment advisor, was to diversify the portfolio by selling a portion of the two original stocks, and to buy stocks in other industries with the proceeds from the sale. The stocks that were purchased paid a higher dividend yield. In addition, call options were sold to generate more income and to hedge against a decline in the value of the portfolio.

Is a broadly diversified portfolio the answer to my stock selection problem?

Once you have chosen the path of broad diversification you reduce your risks of losses, but you may also have to reduce your expected rewards. Your portfolio is overdiversified when you own too many stocks in relation to the size of your account. Should one stock go up sharply, it will have little effect on the total value of your portfolio.

How many different securities should I own in my portfolio?

In a portfolio valued at about $100,000, it is recommended that you buy about 10 securities. Each security should represent approximately 10 percent of the portfolio; however, in larger accounts you should buy approximately

15 to 20 different positions. Each security would then represent about 5 percent to 7 percent of the portfolio.

How should I allocate the assets in my personal account?

It depends on market conditions. When the market is relatively attractive you should invest the bulk of the assets in common stock (subject to your investment objectives). However, if the market reaches a point where the majority of common stocks are fully valued, you should substantially reduce the exposure to common stocks and invest in cash equivalents or short-term bonds.

How should I diversify a bond portfolio?

You should diversify the maturities of the bonds in your portfolio. For example, if you own tax-exempt bonds all maturing in the year 2010, your portfolio is subject to a high degree of interest rate risk. Maturities should be staggered so that part of the portfolio will mature in 1990, 1995, 2000, 2005, and 2010, rather than all maturing in the year 2010.

DOLLAR AVERAGING

Dollar averaging involves the periodic placement (e.g. monthly or quarterly) of equal dollar amounts in securities, regardless of the outlook prevailing at the time the investments are made. Securities might be acquired over a wide range of price levels. Investing equal dollar amounts will buy more shares when prices are low and fewer shares when prices are high.

Dollar averaging is a good strategy for the long-term investor, and for specific objectives such as accumulating the necessary funds to send your children to college. It is also an appropriate strategy as part of your retirement planning.

GOLD AND SILVER

Scarcity, intrinsic beauty, and usefulness of precious metals make gold and silver an investment classic. Ownership of gold and silver has long been a standard of wealth, success, and prudent financial management.

Should I own gold and silver?

Every investor should have a portion of his or her assets in gold and silver. Your attitude toward gold and silver should be the same as the one you have toward fire or life insurance policies. You pay insurance premiums for protection against accidents. The purpose of owning gold and silver is for protection during periods of political and financial uncertainty. It is a hedge against inflation. A strong dollar and perceptions of the future low level of inflation will cause the price of gold and silver to deteriorate. A weak dollar and perceptions of the future high level of inflation will cause the price of gold and silver to rise. The outlook for real interest rates will also influence the price of these metals.

What is the relationship between the prices of gold and silver?

At several points in time, the exchange rate between gold and silver are fixed. It was based on the perceived value of one relative to the other. When the price of silver was pegged at $1.29 per ounce, and gold at $38.00, the price ratio was 29.46 to 1.

Over a long period of time the market price relationship between gold and silver has fluctuated between 19 to 1 and 60 to 1, averaging about 35 to 1. A ratio of 35 to 1 means that you can buy 35 ounces of silver for the same amount of money as 1 ounce of gold.

The following table shows the ratio between the price of gold and the price of silver from 1969 to 1985.

The Ratio of the Price of Gold to the Price of Silver

Year	Ratio Min.	Max.
1969	19	25
1970	19	23
1971	22	31
1972	31	40
1973	33	48
1974	29	43
1975	32	40
1976	22	32
1977	29	35
1978	32	38
1979	19	32
1980	19	38
1981	31	42
1982	40	60
1983	30	46
1984	39	47
1985	48	53
Average	29	40

When the gold-silver ratio falls below 29 to 1, gold is more attractive and you should buy gold. When the price ratio is above 40 to 1, silver is more attractive and you should buy silver instead of gold.

Silver is different from gold since in addition to its speculative appeal it has several industrial uses (photographic materials, electronic products, dentistry, coinage, and jewelry). The world industrial consumption of silver (excluding communist-dominated areas) averaged about 400 million ounces per year from 1974 to 1984.

The price of silver has fluctuated within a narrow price range near $5.00 an ounce from 1974 to 1978. By the end of 1979, the price jumped to $46.00 an ounce, then fell back to $14.00 in 1980. (See graph on opposite page.)

Because we expect the demand for silver to increase faster than supplies, long-term investors should accumu-

SIVER BULLION
PRICE PER
TROY OUNCE
U.S. DOLLARS
(WEEKLY AVERAGES)

late the metal on price weakness. The longer term trend for silver appears to be positive.

GROWTH STOCKS

What is a growth stock?

These are stocks of companies whose sales and earnings are increasing at a faster rate than those of the average company. These companies are often aggressively managed. A large portion of earnings is left in the business and reinvested in research and development, and the introduction of new products and services. In addition, the dividend is usually small.

This management strategy of reinvestment of earnings in a company should, over a long period of time, result in an above-average rate of growth of earnings. Subsequently, it may result in higher prices for the common stock.

After I purchase a growth stock, how long should I keep it?

As an investor in a growth stock, you should be patient. You should take the long-term point of view. It may take many years for the company to grow until it reaches its maturity stage.

CASE IN POINT: Mr. B. bought a common stock of Ralston Purina because he was familiar with their products, Meow Mix and Cat Chow. Since so many people have cats or dogs, Mr. B. felt that consumers would always spend large sums of money to feed their pets. The pet-food industry is sound, stable, and profitable.

After an analysis of the company, Mr. B. bought 1,000 shares of the common stock of Ralston Purina at $10.00 per share. Every morning before breakfast, he would read the financial section of the newspaper to see how his investment was doing. Each day he calculated his unrealized gains or losses.

After two months, the price of Ralston Purina rose to $13.00 per share. His unrealized gain was about $3,000, which amounts to about 30% return on the original $10,000 investment. He was then faced with a problem. Should he or shouldn't he sell the stock? Mr. B. decided to hold on to and watch the price movement of the stock. For about two months more, the stock fluctuated within a narrow price range near $13.00 per share. Mr. B. was tired of watching the stock moving sideways. He decided to sell the stock and nail down his profits. He was happy with his investment results.

Four years later, the price of Ralston Purina reached $45.00 per share. If he had kept his original stock holdings for four more years, rather than sell it, Mr. B. would have realized $35,000 gain on his original $10,000 investment.

Mr. B. learned an important lesson: To be a successful investor, it is important to be patient and to take a long-term point of view.

How much should I pay for a growth stock?

Growth stocks should sell at a higher multiple of price per earnings because of the rapid rate of growth of future earnings. They also often sell at prices well above book value per share. (Book value per share is calculated by taking the total assets and subtracting total liabilities, and then dividing the difference by the number of shares outstanding.) This is justified because of the potential increase in dividends and the expected appreciation in the value of the company. When an average company with stable earnings but with little or no growth potential sells at 8 or 10 times current earnings, usually a growth stock may sell at 20 or 30 times earnings. You should pay more for a growth stock than for a stable stock. However, sometimes these stocks may sell at 50 or 100 times earnings due to probable overoptimism and probable overexpectation. When they reach such a high multiple, you should be very careful and probably avoid the stock, since the downside price risk could be substantial.

SELLING SHORT

When you sell short, you sell a security that you do not own. This is accomplished by borrowing the security that you wish to sell. This borrowing is usually handled by your stockbroker.

Why would I want to sell a security short?

You would sell a security short when you anticipate a decline in its price. You will profit from the short sale when you buy the security (to cover your short) at a lower price than the short sale price.

Short sales against the box (when you already own the underlying security) are carried out to hedge against a possible decline in the price of a security, and also to postpone the taxes associated with the profitable sale of a security. In effect, you delay the payment of taxes by selling short against the box. You do not sell the securities you own; you sell the securities you borrowed. When you decide to sell the securities you own, you buy back (cover your short) the short securities and return the ones you borrowed.

What are the disadvantages of selling short?

When you buy a stock, you can lose 100 percent of your investment, but no more. When you sell short, you can lose much more than 100 percent. For example, let's say you sold short 100 shares at $20, for a net proceed of $2,000. If the stock subsequently rose in price from 20 to 60, you would have to buy it back at one point. If you covered your short at 60, your loss would be $4,000 ($6,000 minus $2,000), or 200 percent on your original short. There would also be a tax disadvantage, since any profits realized from short sales are subject to full, ordinary income tax rate.

Can I sell short in my regular cash account with my broker?

You will have to open a margin account and a short account with your broker. Short sales are subject to margin regulations.

STOP LOSS

We all know that one mistake in the purchase of securities can wipe out the positive effect of many other good investments. To protect your portfolio from a major mistake, a "stop loss" order can be used. This is an order given in advance by you (the investor) to your stockbroker, to sell a stock if its price falls below a predetermined price.

This strategy is useful to prevent you from incurring major losses in the event of an unprecedented decline. But there are also some risks involved. When many investors buy "rising" stocks and try to protect their gains by using similar stop-loss orders, a sharp drop in price could trigger an influx of stop-loss orders within a relatively short period of time. As a result, your shares could be sold at a much lower price than you originally expected. In addition, quite frequently you may be "stopped out" of a stock at a low level. You may later regret making this stop-loss order, because the stock may rise again in price (when you no longer own it).

CASE IN POINT: In mid-1983, the price of Control Data (CDA) reached $64 per share. The company was earning at the rate of $4.20 per share. Cash flow per share reached $9.46. In April of 1985, the stock was recommended by several major brokerage houses near $30 a share. It was selling at a P/E multiple of 7.9, the lowest in the mainframe group. Its earnings were projected to grow at about 14 percent for the next five years. The financial services business (Commercial Credit) was improving as interest rates were falling. At that time, Wall Street anticipated the sale of the company's Commercial Credit operations and a $20 million buyback of its own shares. After analyzing the company's financials, and based on several other experts' recommendations, I bought the stock. The book value per share was near $46. I thought, at that time, that the stock could rise from about $30 per share to about $45 per share (an increase of about 50 percent). On September 12, 1985, an announcement was published in the financial papers indicating Control Data was selling $200 million worth of 14¾ percent Subordinated Notes due September 1, 1995. The underwriters were Goldman, Sachs & Co. and Merrill Lynch Capital Markets. Several days later, this offer was suddenly withdrawn. The stock of Control Data tumbled. By mid-October of 1985, it had dropped to $18 per share. The common shares were trading at almost one-third of the current estimated book value. I lost almost 50 percent on my investment. I should have used the "stop-loss rule" to cut my losses immediately when the situation changed.

Most technicians use stop-losses as a routine strategy. A breakout above resistance triggers a buy and a breakdown below support triggers a sell. These entries and exits are a result of an error. However, a worse error is failing to stop your loss. Ignoring new evidence that you were wrong in judgement, or insisting on fighting a trend, could be very costly. Emotionally, it is very difficult to admit a mistake. But from an investment point of view, it is even more painful to watch your investments erode.

RISK/REWARD RATIO

The final step in any investment decision should be a review of the risk/reward ratio. You should compare the potential risk against the potential reward for each investment. You should also estimate the risk/reward ratio for the overall market at the time an investment is made. For example, try to project the number of points that the Dow Jones Industrial could decline against the number of points that the Dow could rise. The comparison of the upside potential (in percentage) with the downside risk (in percentage) should give you a good picture of the relative attractiveness of your investment.

DISCOUNTING THE BAD/GOOD MARKET NEWS

There is a saying on Wall Street, "Buy on bad news, and sell on good news." The stock market is a discounting mechanism. It discounts news in advance. By the time the news is out, stock prices have probably already reacted to it. For that reason, an investment strategy of doing the opposite to the reported news may prove to be prudent.

Stockbrokers and investment advisors will tell you that when the majority of their customers call and tell them to sell stocks because of bad news — this is probably the best time to buy. The same holds true in reverse, when the majority of customers put pressure on brokers and advisors to be fully invested because of good news. This is probably the time to do some selling.

Impending events — economic, political, or other — have a direct effect on the stock market. If an event is anticipated and well-advertised and discussed in the media, by the time the event actually occurs and the news is out, it is no longer significant as far as the stock market is concerned. The market mechanism has discounted the news. For example, if the President of the United States were to die unexpectedly, there would be a swift and significant response on the stock market. A Presidential election would be less likely to affect the market significantly, as such an event would have been widely publicized and analyzed for months in advance.

TOTAL RETURN CONCEPT

The total return concept means that you look for several sources of income on your investments. This usually includes income from interest, dividends, capital gains, and option premiums.

Many investment strategies are limited only to one source of income. For example, a growth stock that pays no dividends and has no listed options, could benefit you only if it goes up in price. This will result in capital gains (one source of income). Or, suppose you own a bond that pays interest but its price changes only minimally over an extended period of time. You will benefit only from the interest. The concept of total return is to select these investments that could generate both dividend and capital gain and option premiums, the sum of which should not only be higher but also more consistent over a period of time than other alternative investments. For example, if you can make 8 percent from dividends, 8 percent from capital gains, and 8 percent from options premium, the total annual return will equal 24 percent.

How long will it take to double my money?

If you invest $100,000 with a 10 percent annual return (after tax), it will take 7.2 years to double your money to $200,000. Without using sophisticated computers, you can use a simple rule known as Rule 72: Divide 0.72 years by the annual percentage rate of return of your investment. The answer will give you approximately the number of years required to double your investment. This rule assumes that interest is compounded annually. An investment will double in a shorter period of time if interest is compounded daily or monthly.

The following table shows that as the annual rate of return rises, you need less number of years to double your investment.

Annual rate of return	Number of years to double
0.08	0.72 yrs. / 0.08 = 9.0 yrs.
0.09	0.72 yrs. / 0.09 = 8.0 yrs.
0.10	0.72 yrs. / 0.10 = 7.2 yrs.
0.11	0.72 yrs. / 0.11 = 6.5 yrs.
0.12	0.72 yrs. / 0.12 = 6.0 yrs.
0.13	0.72 yrs. / 0.13 = 5.5 yrs.
0.14	0.72 yrs. / 0.14 = 5.1 yrs.
0.15	0.72 yrs. / 0.15 = 4.8 yrs.

CHAPTER 4

Options
Hedging Strategies

This chapter is divided into several sections: The first deals with call options, the second with put options, the third with spreads and straddles, and the fourth covers miscellaneous points to consider in option trading. The objectives, risks, obligations, advantages, and disadvantages of each are explained. Many investors are confused about some of the technical aspects of option trading. Some of the most common questions raised by concerned investors are discussed throughout.

SELLING OPTIONS — A USEFUL
INVESTMENT TOOL

Selling options is a useful, conservative tool for investors who wish to make money and keep it, accumulate wealth and preserve it. You may be an investor who regards option writing as only an occasional adjunct to your overall investment program. Or, you may be an investor who purchases particular stocks for your pension fund or profit sharing plan, for the specific purpose of continuously writing options against them. Selling options is a tool that can help you and your organization achieve specific investment goals and improve your overall investment performance.

CALL OPTIONS

A Historical Perspective

Is selling options a new idea?

Selling options is not a new idea. Options have been bought and sold in the United States for more than a century, and even longer in Europe, but it was only with the establishment of the Chicago Board Options Exchange that a very broad market was established.

Until 1973, option trading was strictly an over-the-counter business conducted by a few firms that specialized in the field. It was a custom market. Each contract was unique and each writer had to search for a buyer seeking that particular option.

The CBOE was incorporated as a legally separate and independent nonprofit membership corporation. It is registered as a national securities exchange with the Securities and Exchange Commission of the United States. The Options Exchange opened trading on April 26, 1973, with only 16 stocks listed. It began as the world's first and only exchange established expressly for trading in stock options — a distinction it still holds.

Since trading in standardized options began on organized exchanges, there has been a growing recognition of their effectiveness as anti-speculative, risk-limiting and return-enhancing investment vehicles that also help protect profits in stocks already owned.

What is an "option?"

Webster defines an option as "a stipulated privilege of buying and selling a stated property, service or commodity at a given price within a specified time." An option is a contract allowing its holder to buy from an investor or to sell to another investor, 100 shares of a stock at a specified price (exercise price) within a specified time (expiration date).

What is a "call option?"

Call (option) is an option contract giving its owner (holder) the right to buy a specific number of shares of a specified stock for a specified price (striking price) on or before a specified expiration date.

As a seller of call options, you receive a payment known as a premium. You sell contracts granting the buyer the right to buy shares of common stock, for a specified time at a specified price. They are referred to as calls because they allow the owner of the call option to exercise his or her right to "call away" the stock from its owner.

SELLING CALL OPTIONS — FOUR MAIN OBJECTIVES

What are the specific objectives of selling call options?

1. To receive additional income on the stocks in your portfolio. This additional income is equal to the amount of premium received

2. To protect your portfolio against loss of capital during declining markets. You reduce the downside risk inherent in owning common stocks. It is a way to "hedge" your securities against a possible decline in the market. Your risk reduction is equal to the amount of premium received.

3. To achieve a more stable and consistent investment performance over a long period of time. This is achieved by reducing the price volatility of the portfolio using option hedging strategies.

4. To increase the total return on investment (dividend income plus options premium plus, if exercised, capital gain) while avoiding excessive risk.

For example: Let us say that you purchased a stock at $18, and then you sold a three-month call option for $1 for which you received $100. You entered into an obligation to deliver your stock at $20. (Striking price is $20.) You received an additional $100 immediately. If your stock declines to $17, you did not lose anything. You reduced your downside risk by $100. You can sell call options several times a year. You could receive $100 once every three months. Your maximum profit is limited should your stock increase sharply, but you reduce your downside risk too. You will achieve a more stable return on your investment. Your total return is now generated from three sources of income — dividend income, options premium, and (if exercised) capital gain income. You obtain "above-the-market" selling price for the stock. If you attempted to sell the stock at $20, you actually sold it for $21 ($20 + $1.00 premium income).

COVERED CALL OPTIONS

A covered option writer is the seller of an option who owns the underlying security covered by the option as long as he remains obligated as the writer. In exchange for the premium he receives, the "covered writer" subjects himself to the full risk of decline in value of the underlying stock. At the same time, he also gives up the opportunity for gain resulting from a possible increase in the price (above the exercise price).

WHAT TO CONSIDER WHEN SELLING CALL OPTIONS

As the seller of a call option, you must understand the following four considerations:

1. Your obligation
2. Your rights under current laws
3. The risks
4. How and when you receive dividends

Let's examine each of these areas more closely.

1. Obligations

What are my obligations as a seller of a call option

As a seller of a call (through your broker), you assumed an obligation to sell the underlying security upon assignment to you of an exercise notice. This obligation continues until you close your position in the option. For each option contract, you are responsible for delivering 100 shares of the underlying security at the price specified in the option contract during the term of the option. The number of shares and option striking price may change based upon changes such as stock splits, reverse splits, stock dividends, rights and/or warrants offerings, or other similar action by the issuer.

After I sell a call option, can I release myself from the obligation to sell the stock at the option striking price?

You release your obligation by buying back the call option in the open market.

2. Rights

What are my rights as a seller of call options?

As a seller of call options, your rights are subject to the bylaws and rules of the Options Clearing Corporation, and the constitutions and rules of the exchanges on which the options are traded. You are paid a premium at the time you sell the call. The money you receive is yours. You can take it out of your broker's account or reinvest it. As long as you own the underlying stock, you have the right to receive dividends.

3. Risks

What are my risks in selling covered call options against a stock in my portfolio?

As a seller of a covered call option you own the underlying stock. As long as you own the stock you are subject to the full risk of any stockholder. In exchange for the premium received, so long as you remain the writer of an option, you have given up the opportunity for a gain resulting from an increase in the price of the underlying security above the exercise price. In the event that a secondary market in an option ceases to exist, closing transactions may not be possible. If exercise restrictions are also imposed while there is no secondary market, options may be unable to be either sold or exercised. You may not be able to "buy in" an option.

If a broker handling your option account becomes insolvent or otherwise ceases to do business, you may not be able to sell or exercise options held in your account, and your position as a writer of options may be liquidated.

What are the disadvantages of selling call options against stock in my portfolio?

Your potential profit as the owner of the underlying stock is limited, since you would not benefit from a sharp rise in the price of the stock. The premium you receive is considered ordinary income for tax purposes. The premium received might be very small (especially in a depressed market). Commission expenses may reduce your net profits.

If you expect a sudden rise in the price of a stock, you should not sell the call options, because you will have to buy the calls back at a higher price when you wish to sell the underlying stock.

Are there risks in selling uncovered calls?

When you sell uncovered calls, you should compare the high potential risks against the limited potential rewards. When you sell an uncovered call you do not own the underlying stock. Your loss potential is unlimited. You should consider what will happen when the underlying stock rises sharply and the call is exercised. You will have to buy the underlying stock (at much higher prices) in the open market to make delivery. For that reason you could realize a large loss. On the other hand, when you sell an uncovered call your profit potential is limited to the premium received. The value of your short call cannot decline to below zero.

4. Dividends

Do I continue to receive dividends when I sell call options?

Yes. You continue to receive dividends as long as you own the stock.

Is it important to watch for ex-dividend dates?

Yes. You should watch for ex-dividend dates, especially in the case of high-paying dividend stock. The owner of the call may exercise the option just prior to ex-dividend dates, for the purpose of collecting the dividend. The specialist on an exchange may buy an "in-the-money" call with an intrinsic value, just for the purpose of exercising the call, and become the owner of the stock just for the purpose of receiving the dividend.

As a holder of a call, when am I entitled to the cash dividend on the underlying stock?

You will be entitled to the cash dividend if on the day prior to ex-dividend date you tender an exercise notice.

> **If ABC corporation pays a 50 percent stock dividend and I own one call option with a strike price of 30, what will happen to my call?**

You will now own one option for 150 shares, with a new strike price of 20.

BEHAVIOR OF OPTION PRICES

> **How are option prices determined, and why do they fluctuate so much?**

Option prices are the premiums the buyer pays to acquire the option, and which the writer receives for selling the option. The premium is the aggregate price of an option, agreed upon between the buyer and writer, or their agents, in a transaction on the floor of an exchange. The buyer pays a premium and a commission to a broker; the seller receives the premium minus the commission. The premium level is determined at the exchange auction market by supply and demand, the amount of time remaining in the option, its exercise price, and the market price of the underlying stock.

The premium is an extremely important factor in the success or failure of a particular option strategy and in the resulting total rate of return on investor's option strategy and in the resulting total rate of return on investor's capital. Low premium will benefit the buyer; high premium will benefit the seller.

THE LEVEL OF OPTION PREMIUMS

> **How is the amount of option premium determined?**

The amount of premium paid by buyers of options and received by you as a seller of options is determined at the exchange auction by supply and demand forces.

Premiums will go up and down with market fluctuations. When the market is depressed, usually near a bottom, premiums are relatively low. When the market is strong, or near a top, demand for options is high, and premiums are relatively high.

Premiums are also a function of stock volatility. This volatility is measured in terms of (percent) change in price during a day or a week. Traders often consider a stock volatile, if the (percent) change during any week exceeded 5 percent. Premiums on volatile stocks are much higher than premiums on stable stocks.

When can you withdraw from your account the premium income from the sale of a call?

You may withdraw the entire premium immediately if, for example, you own 100 shares of the underlying stock in your cash account, the stock is selling at 30, and you sold one call with a strike price of 30.

I purchased the ABC stock at 23 in June, and sold a December 25 call option in October. The stock rose to 26 (one point above the strike price). Will I get exercised immediately as soon as the price of the stock rose above the strike price?

The owner of the call usually waits until expiration day. However, the owner of a call, just prior to ex-dividend day, may call for the stock so that he can receive the dividend.

VALUE OF OPTIONS

What is the fair value of an option?

The fair value of an option may be less than, equal to, or greater than its market value. It is based on one's subjective judgement of an option's worth under efficient market condition. Computerized "Relative Value Reports" are available and are used by many professionals as a guide, but skepticism often exists about the meaning of the value concept. An option can be considered "undervalued," but if the stock goes down the option becomes valueless.

Likewise, an option can be considered "overvalued," but if the stock goes up the value of the option will continue to go up.

What is the relationship between time and the value of options?

On expiration day an option has no time value. A six-month option has more time value than a three-month option. The "time value" of options declines as the options get closer to maturity. For example: When ABC stock is trading at $33 and the October 30 call is trading at $4¼, the time value of the call is $1¼ and the intrinsic value is $3. Time value is variable and is a function of what buyers and sellers expect the price of the underlying stock to do during the time left to expiration date.

OUT-OF-THE-MONEY CALL OPTIONS

An out-of-the-money call option is an option for which the exercise price is above the current market price of the stock. For example, if the stock is currently selling at $32 and the call option has an exercise price of $35, the call option is out-of-the-money by $3.

What are the reasons for selling out-of-the-money call options?

Selling calls above current price levels is "programmed selling" above current prices. To a certain degree it solves the emotional problem of selling into strength. When you sell an out-of-the-money call, the probability that the stock will be taken away from you is relatively small. Therefore, very often the stock is not exercised and as a seller of the call you will keep the premium and the stock because the stock was not exercised. Selling out-of-the-money calls (if exercised) will generate income from three sources: dividend income, plus option income, plus capital gains.

IN-THE-MONEY CALL OPTIONS

What are in-the-money call options?

An in-the-money call option is an option whose exercise price is below the current market price of the underlying stock. For example, when the market price of a stock is 30, and the call option has a striking price of 25, the call option is in-the-money 5 points. If the option is exercised immediately, this 5-point value can be realized.

When should I sell in-the-money call options?

You should sell in-the-money call options when you expect the market to go down. Selling the in-the-money call will generate high cash flow because of higher option premiums. The value of the calls will decline when the market declines and they hopefully could be bought back at a lower price.

TIMING OF THE SALE OF CALL OPTIONS

When is it advisable to sell call options against stocks in my portfolio?

It is advisable to sell call options against stocks in your portfolio:

When you expect the stock in your portfolio to show little or no price change over the life of the call option.

When the underlying stock has reached its resistance level.

When the market has reached an overbought condition.

When both short-term and intermediate trends are up, but at the same time, negative technical alerts (volume alert, price alert, or exhaustion gap) are signaled.

When you have a bullish attitude toward the underlying issue, and look for less potential capital gains from stock appreciation, but wish to increase current income from option premium.

BUYING CALL OPTIONS

For every seller of calls there must be a buyer of calls. For a transaction to be consummated, both the seller and buyer must be satisfied. "Why would anyone buy my calls?" is a very frequent question.

What are the objectives of buying a call option?

As a call option buyer you hope that the price of the option will go up, due to increase in price of the underlying stock, within a relatively short time. If the price of the underlying stock declines, as an option buyer you may lose the entire premium investment. However, in a sharply declining market this loss (of the entire premium) could be smaller than the possible loss incurred in owning the underlying stock. For that reason, forecasting short-term price trends of the underlying stock is of great importance in call option buying.

What are the advantages of buying a call?

Buying a call option requires a small investment. The cost of the option is only a small fraction of the cost of the stock. (Especially in "out-of-the-money calls.") The rate of return on your investment can be considerably higher than the rate of return generated when you buy a stock outright. Your risk is limited to the cost of the call option. As a buyer of the call option you know in advance your maximum possible loss.

What are the risks involved in buying a call option?

As a buyer of an option you should be aware that your total potential loss is limited to the cost of the premium paid for the option. Should the option expire unexercised you could lose the entire premium. You also assume the risk of losing part of the premium paid, if the underlying stock rises, but not enough to recover your cost of the call.

What are my rights as a holder of a call?

As a holder of a call you have the right to purchase the underlying security covered by the option at the stated exercise price, at any time prior to the expiration of the option. This can be done by instructing your broker to exercise your call option. An option that expires unexercised becomes worthless. The holder of a call option can liquidate his position in the secondary market by a closing sale transaction.

PUT OPTIONS

What is a put option?

A put option is an option contract giving its owner the right to sell a specific number of shares for a specified price on or before an expiration date. For example: Jan 35 Put Option for Allied Corp. means that the option to sell 100 shares of Allied Corp. expires in January and the exercise price is $35 a share. One put is a contract for 100 shares (10 puts is a contract for 1,000 shares).

WHY USE PUT OPTIONS?

What are the objectives of selling put options?

The objectives of selling put options are: (a) to receive a premium, and (b) to plan the buying of the underlying common stock, at prices below current market prices.

What are the rights of the writer (the seller) of a put option?

The seller of a put has the right to receive the premium proceeds as soon as the sale transaction clears.

PUT OPTIONS OBLIGATIONS

What is my obligation as a put writer (seller)?

You must buy the stock at the exercise price, but your cost is reduced by the amount of put premium you receive.

What is my obligation as a put buyer?

As a put buyer, you have to pay the option premium.

After I sell a put, how can I be released from my obligation to buy the stock?

You can buy back the put in the open market or you can roll over the put for another 3 or 6 months by buying back (covering) your existing put and selling a new put.

DEEP-IN-THE-MONEY PUT OPTIONS

What are the reasons for selling "deep-in-the-money" put options?

To keep a short-term loss from developing into a long-term loss you can sell the underlying stock to realize the short-term loss and simultaneously write a deep-in-the-money put. The put is nearly certain to be exercised.

The premium received from the sale of a deep-in-the-money put is relatively large. If the stock rises above the exercise price you keep the premium proceeds and you will not get exercised.

DISADVANTAGES OF PUT OPTIONS

What are the disadvantages of selling put options?

They are similar to the sale of covered call options. Should the stock go up above the exercise price, your income is limited to the premium received. Should the stock go down, your loss is identical to the one experienced by the owner of the stock.

ADVANTAGES OF PUT OPTIONS

What are the advantages of selling put options?

The seller of the put does not have to lay out any cash. In fact, the seller receives cash in the form of an option premium. He or she may post Treasury securities as collateral (or Money Market funds) and continues to receive interest income on these collaterals.

What are the reasons for buying a put option?

You buy a put option when you expect the price of the put option to rise. The increase in the price of a put takes place when the price of the underlying stock declines.

You can also buy a put to protect an unrealized profit in your current stock position; to avoid selling a stock on which you have a capital gain but guarantee a selling price as long as the put option is outstanding; or to participate in an additional capital gain in the stock if it continues to rise.

What are the advantages of buying a put in comparison to selling short?

Buying a put has the following advantages: It has a lower loss potential. Your potential loss is limited to your cost of the put. For example; if you bought 10 puts for $2 each, your cost is $2,000 and your maximum potential loss is $2,000. The purchase of a put requires a smaller capital commitment than selling short the stock. It does not require waiting for an uptick in the stock.

PUT OPTION PREMIUMS

How is the level of option premium determined?

The option premium, paid by the buyer of the option and received by the seller of the option, is one of the most important considerations in option trading. The premium at any given time is determined by forces of supply and demand for the option. Often when a stock has an extended decline, interest in buying puts by speculators is going up and the put premium will go up too. When a stock has an extended rise, interest in buying puts by speculators diminishes and put premiums go down.

When is the put option premium received?

You, as an option seller, receive the premium as soon as the option transaction clears.

TIME VALUE OF OPTIONS

How is the time value of the option determined?

Option is a "wasting" asset. It becomes worthless on expiration date. As the expiration date gets closer, the time value of the option decreases. The less time remaining until the expiration date, the lower the premium will be.

A COMBINATION STRATEGY — SELLING A STOCK AND SELLING A PUT OPTION

What is the reason for selling a stock I own, and simultaneously selling a put option?

You can re-establish a stock position at a lower price with a put option. Suppose you decide to sell a stock in fear of a price decline or to generate cash to reduce margin, but you want to re-establish your position in the stock at a later date; you can do this very effectively by selling puts. For example: you own a stock at 30 for over a year and it appreciates to 40. You anticipate a price decline but you want to establish a long-term capital gain. You like the stock, but you wish to re-establish your position, if possible, at a lower level. You can sell the stock and simultaneously sell a 35 strike price put. If the stock continues to go up, you realize your 10 points capital gain (40-30), plus the put premium received (short-term capital gain). If the stock goes down, you realize your capital gain, but you would also take possession of the stock at a lower price (in our example, 35 minus the premium received). You generate cash from the sale of the stock, which could be used to reduce your margin, or for other investments.

SELLING PUTS — A CONSERVATIVE STRATEGY

Is selling a put option a conservative strategy?

Yes. Selling a put option is a very conservative strategy. It is an alternative to buying or owning the stock. You sell put options in stocks that you wish to purchase anyhow. As a potential investor in the underlying stock, you would like the price of the stock to decline so that you will be able to buy the stock at lower prices.

SPREADS

Call Spreads

How can I profit from a call spread?

When you buy the lower exercise price and sell the higher exercise price, you establish a bull call spread. Since the lower exercise price costs you more than the proceeds from the sale of the higher exercise price, you establish a net debit. You expect the spread to widen. You expect the call you bought to go up in price and the call you sold to go down in price.

Put Spreads

What is a bearish spread?

A spread written for a net debit would be bearish because you buy the upper strike and sell the lower strike. In a case of a put, the upper strike price has the larger premium and the lower strike price has the lower premium.

In a bearish spread you always buy the upper strike and sell the lower strike.

What are the advantages and disadvantages of spreads?

Using spreads reduces your risk exposure, but this is achieved at the expense of limiting your profit potential.

Index Futures Spreads

A futures contract is an agreement to buy or sell a specific "commodity" at a predetermined price on a future date. That commodity can be, for example, gold, silver, sugar, Treasury bills, or a stock index. A stock index represents the value of the underlying issues of stock that make up the index. In November 1985, 14 market and industry indices existed:

Market Indices

Major Market Index (XMI)
AMEX Market Value Index (XAM)
NYSE Composite Index (NYA)
NYSE Double Index (NDX)
Technology Index (PSE)
S&P 100 (OEX)
S&P 500 (SPX)
Value Line Composite Index (XVL)
National O-T-C 100 Index (XOC)
NASDAQ-100 Index (NDQ)

Industry Indices

Computer Technology Index (XCI)
Oil Index (XOI)
Gold/Silver Index (XAU)
Transportation Index (XTI)

Although trading futures contracts is considered a game for high-rollers, trading futures spreads is a conservative approach to trading. In a futures spread you simultaneously buy one futures contract and sell another. For example:

Buy one NYSE (New York Stock Exchange) Composite Index December futures contract (YXZ), and
Sell one Major Market Index November futures contract (MXX).

The spread trader focuses on the dollar value of the spread, which can either widen or decrease. For example, if you purchase one contract for $2,000, and sell another contract for $1,900, your cost for the spread is $100. (This is the difference between the purchase cost and the proceeds from the sale.) You hope that the spread will widen. When the spread increases in value to $150, you can close your position and your profit will amount to $50. This will happen when, for example, the contract you bought rose to $2,100 and the contract you sold increased to $1,950. Your profit in the spread is $50 ($150 proceeds from the sale at the closing minus $100 the cost of your spread).

STRADDLES

What is a straddle?

A straddle is the purchase of a call and the purchase of a put at the same striking price. For example, when you buy a 50 call and you buy a 50 put you establish a straddle. If you buy a 50 call and buy a 60 put (different striking prices) you establish a combination.

What is the best option strategy when I do not anticipate that the stock price will change?

A speculator who does not expect the price of a stock to change in the immediate future will sell an uncovered straddle. It involves the sale of a call and the sale of a put. The investor will receive income from two premiums — the call and the put. You should buy a straddle when you anticipate substantial fluctuations in the price of a stock.

DOWN-AND-OUT OPTION

What is a down-and-out option?

A down-and-out option is an option which has an expiration price as well as an expiration date. For example, an investor buys a six-month down-and-out option covering a specific number of shares of a stock. Exercise price is 50, expiration price is 45. If the market price falls below 45 on any day within the six months (and the option is not exercised) the option holder loses his option and the premium paid. The price expiration feature makes the option more attractive to a writer because his obligation might terminate prior to the six-month expiration date. Therefore, he usually is willing to accept a smaller premium.

OTHER POINTS TO CONSIDER IN OPTIONS TRADING

If trading has been halted in an underlying stock, which option orders can be executed?

You can only cancel a former order. You cannot place GTC, limit, or market orders.

Are commission costs in options trading prohibitive for small investors?

If you buy or sell a small number of call or put options, the commission costs could be very high relative to the amount of money involved. For example, you may sell two calls for a $1 premium, which will gross you $200, but your broker may charge a minimum commission of $30.

The commission cost represents 15 percent of the transaction. These transaction costs may absorb a significant part of your options gains. You should look for a broker who will charge you a lower commission rate, without sacrificing the quality of the service.

Can I buy listed options on margin?

No. You cannot buy options on margin.

What does it mean when I open a discretionary account with a broker?

You give the broker discretion to buy or to sell as to time, price, security, number of shares, and number of options. The issuing corporation cannot sell its own options.

Can I trade any other type of options besides equity options?

Yes. There are options on foreign currencies, interest rates, and various indices. This is a very specialized field, so you may want to consult an expert before attempting to trade on your own.

A Prudent Man Rule

Is option writing a prudent investment strategy?

Yes. A reasonably prudent man or woman should look for an investment that provides a reasonable income at a reasonable risk.

In general, covered call writing fits comfortably within the guidelines of trust law principles because such transactions tend to both preserve capital and make the property more productive. A security held in a portfolio will do one of three things: it may increase in value, decrease in value, or remain unchanged. It can be argued that under any of these circumstances, writing calls on portfolio securities may be prudent. If the stock goes up in price, the only sacrifice made by the writer is an opportunity for even greater profits. If assets are not held for speculation and the highest profit, this possibility may be irrelevant. If the stock declines in value, writing covered calls on the stock reduces the loss which would have been incurred on the underlying stock had the calls not been written. Therefore, such an investment technique may act to conserve principal. If the price of the stock remains constant, the premium income adds to the yield on the investment thus increasing the total return on your investment. For these reasons, the prudence of covered call writing is gradually becoming recognized.

Which option strategies have been approved under ERISA as being prudent?

ERISA is concerned with the protection of employees who are covered by pension plans. Writing covered calls and writing puts against cash have been approved under ERISA as being prudent.

CHAPTER **5**

Market Timing Indicators and Technical Analysis

TIMING INDICATORS — A USEFUL
INVESTMENT TOOL

Accurate timing is a key element to successful investing. When you buy a "good" stock, you may still lose money if you buy it at the "wrong" time. Yet, you may buy a speculative stock with poor fundamentals but still make money if your timing is right.

Although many academicians claim that the stock market and securities often fluctuate randomly, it is wrong to conclude that this is always the case. Many professionals know that under specific extreme conditions, certain price moves can be predicted with some degree of certainty. You can separate the nonrandom from random moves by using historically tested market timing indicators to help improve your investment decisions.

ADVANCES MINUS DECLINES ISSUES DAILY CUMULATIVE

This indicator (also known as Market Breadth) measures the number of advancing stocks minus the number of declining stocks. The cumulative line is calculated daily. When advances exceed declines the breadth is positive. When declines exceed advances the breadth is negative. The net positive or negative cumulative is added to the cumulative of the previous week. This indicator measures the overall market performance. The trend of the Dow Jones Industrials is compared to the trend of the advances minus declines cumulative. If the breadth is neutral when the Dow Industrials is up, the conclusion is that the market advance (rally) will not be sustained. It is believed that the breadth has to participate in the market move if the rally is to be sustained.

ADVANCE-DECLINE RATIO (SEVEN-DAY)

This breadth measure is calculated by dividing the total number of issues advancing on the New York Stock Exchange by the total number of issues declining during the last seven days. It is useful in pinpointing short-term trend reversals.

When the ratio exceeds 1.50, it is believed that the market is near a short-term top (is overbought). When the ratio is below 0.66, it is believed that the market is near a short-term bottom (is oversold).

BARRON'S CONFIDENCE INDEX

This index is a ratio of high-quality bonds yields to speculative bonds yields. It is based on the theory that informed, sophisticated investors act far ahead of the general public. They seek safety in higher grade bonds during unfavorable market periods. A flow of funds into lower grade bonds indicates a bullish attitude. When the index is below 87 it is bullish. When the index is near 94 it is bearish. For example, in 1982, near the market bottom, Barron's Confidence Index declined to 85 percent.

BOND YIELD/FEDERAL FUND RATE RATIO

The Federal Reserve has the power to influence the economy through changes in monetary policy. Its influence on economic activity indirectly affects the stock market. When federal fund rates go down, the Federal Reserve is increasing the money supply and easing monetary policy. This is bullish for the stock market. When federal fund rates go up, the Federal Reserve is tightening monetary policy and this is bearish for the stock market.

When the ratio of bond yield to federal fund rate is below 1.00, the environment for stocks is negative and bearish. When the ratio is above 1.00, the environment for stock is positive and bullish.

Another monetary indicator, the AAA bonds/13-Week T-Bills, is very similar in its behavior to the bond yield/federal fund rate ratio indicator.

CASH POSITION OF MUTUAL FUNDS

This indicator measures the potential of buying power of mutual funds. It is the ratio of highly liquid assets (cash, U.S. government securities) to total assets. For example, if the liquid assets for any given month were $6 billion and the total net assets were $50 billion, the monthly ratio would be 0.12 (or 12 percent). It shows the relative level of buying power available for investment by mutual funds.

A decline in the cash position indicates that the investment managers' psychology is too complacent. Because of their optimistic outlook, the managers have committed their cash to the stock market. Similarly, an increase in the cash position (due to heavy selling or lack of buying) indicates that investment managers are worried. Because of their pessimistic outlook, they keep a relatively high percentage of their portfolios in cash reserves. An increase in the cash reserve increases their potential buying power.

A ratio of 8 percent or less is bearish, because the cash reserve is too low to support a sustained market advance. A ratio of 12 percent or more is bullish, because it shows that there is ample cash to buy stocks. A ratio near 10 percent is considered neutral. Historically, this indicator has fluctuated within a 5 percent - 14 percent range. Near the 1970 and 1974 stock market bottom this ratio reached 13 percent. Near the 1982 bottom it was near 14.3 percent. Near the 1961 and 1968 stock market top the ratio was near 5 percent. Mutual funds need to keep some reserve to allow for sudden redemptions. A cash position of 5 percent is practically a fully invested position.

DOW THEORY

What is the Dow Theory, and how can I use it as a market timing tool?

The Dow Theory derives its name from Charles Dow, born in 1851 and founder of Dow Jones & Company. The purpose of the Dow Theory is to identify major changes in market direction. The theory states that when both the Dow Jones Industrial Average (DJIA) and the DJ Transportation Average break into new highs, a bullish trend is confirmed. When the Industrial and Transportation Averages break through new low points, in previously declining markets, a bearish trend is confirmed. However, when the DJIA breaks to a new high and the DJ Transportation Average does not, it confirms that the uptrend in the DJIA will not be sustained. The same is true on the downside.

FOREIGN MARKETS' FINANCIAL INDEXES

Foreign markets' indexes often lead the U.S. markets. For example, in 1968 the London market stopped rising six months before the U.S. market stopped. In 1972

London stocks peaked approximately eight months before the U.S. market peaked.

STOCK INDEX FUTURES SENTIMENT INDEX

This index is derived weekly by compiling the opinions of a sample of futures traders and analysts. When the bullish consensus reaches 75 percent or above, the market is usually near a peak. When the bullish consensus reaches 30 percent or below, the market is near a bottom.

GENERAL MOTORS "BELLWETHER" THEORY

This theory holds that when General Motors stock is in a rising pattern and four months elapse without a new high for the stock, this constitutes a critical warning signal for the whole market.

When GM shares are in a downtrend and four months pass without a new low, the odds favor higher prices for the whole market. The Bellwether theory is not infallible. In 1974 it flashed a "buy" signal that was too early and whipsawed its followers for months in a plunging stock market.

HIGH-LOW DIFFERENTIAL (DAILY)

The number of stocks reaching new highs minus the number of stocks reaching new lows on the NYSE is calculated daily. This difference describes the strength or the weakness of the overall market. When the 10-day moving average of the difference is above the 30-day moving average, this indicator is favorable.

INDICATOR DIGEST SHORT-TERM TRADING GUIDE (SGA)

SGA stands for "speculative group activity." The theory behind this indicator is that if the speculative trading favorites start to display real activity in a new direction, the rest of the market is not far behind.

This indicator was originally developed by Indicator Digest (one of the pioneers in the analysis of technical indicators) to help investors who trade the shorter-term swings (swings occurring within a few weeks or a few months).

INSIDER TRANSACTIONS
(Selling and Buying by Three or More Insiders)

Who is considered an insider?

The Securities and Exchange Commission defines "insiders" as officers, directors, and major shareholders of publicly owned corporations. Insiders as a group have a major advantage over public investors. They are far closer to their company than any securities analyst can possibly be, and they are often in a better position to judge their company's longer-term prospects, as well. Insiders often have prior knowledge of important developments that may affect a company's stock price. The insider sales/purchase ratio is measured by the ratio of the number of insider sales to purchases. It describes the buying and selling decisions of insiders. Insiders sell more as the market rises and less as the market falls. Near a market top there is a high level of insider selling with little insider buying.

When the eight-week average of insider sales/purchases ratio is equal to 2.0, this indicator is considered neutral. When the ratio is below 1.3, it is considered to be bullish, while a ratio above 2.8 tends to be bearish. This indicator often leads the market.

Although an insider may sell a stock because cash is needed to pay a mortgage or a college tuition, more often the reason for the sale is an awareness of a deterioration in the business condition. This information may not be available at that time to the public. Insiders often buy their company's stock when they feel that it is undervalued.

How can I benefit from information regarding the buying and selling patterns of corporate insiders?

By law insiders must report transactions in their own company to the Securities and Exchange Commission (SEC). Stocks in which there have been three insider sellers within a three-month period, but no insider buyers, rise less than the market during market advances. They decline by greater amounts during market declines. Stocks in which there has been buying by at least three insiders within a three-month period — and no sellers — outperform the market on upswings. They also decline less than most stocks during market downswings.

MARGIN LEVEL INDICATOR

In a bull market, margin level usually increases as stock prices go up. When a divergence occurs, the prices start to decline; if the margin continues to rise, this indicator gives a bearish signal.

MOMENTUM INDICATORS

Momentum indicators are generally related to price and volume behavior. They attempt to determine the underlying strength or weakness of market trends and to identify overbought and oversold market conditions.

Volume momentum indicators are based on the assumption that a change in volume is a prerequisite to a change in price. For that reason, an increase in volume often precedes an increase in price in the marketplace. After the market has risen for some time, a decline in volume may indicate that a change in price trend is imminent. A sharp decline in volume after the market has been declining for some time indicates that the emotional selling (which usually takes place near the end of a downtrend) has been completed, and that prices will soon start rising.

Price momentum indicators measure the difference between the closing price of the Dow Jones Industrial Average and its 30-day average price. When the difference is about +5 percent, the market is overbought. When the difference is -5 percent, the market is oversold.

MOST ACTIVE STOCKS RATIO

The 10 most active stocks on the NYSE represent less than one-quarter of 1 percent of the total number of shares listed. Yet they can often represent up to 10 percent of the total daily volume of trading on the NYSE. For that reason, an analysis of the most active stocks could reveal what the large institutions are doing.

Each week the 20 most active stocks are examined. This is done by dividing the number of advancing stocks by the total number of advancing and declining stocks. The ratio is then averaged over the latest 10-week period.

This indicator is used to determine overbought and oversold market conditions. When the ratio exceeds 60 percent, it indicates an overbought market. When the ratio drops below 30 percent, it indicates an oversold market condition.

PERCENTAGE OF NYSE STOCKS ABOVE THEIR 10-WEEK MOVING AVERAGE

This is a weekly tally of the percentage of stocks above their 10-week moving average, also known as a diffusion index. This percentage tends to change direction ahead of the overall market. Termination of price uptrend is signaled when the percentage rises above 70 percent, 80 percent, or 90 percent, depending upon the strength of the bull market in progress; termination of downtrend is signaled when the percentage drops below 30 percent, 20 percent, or 10 percent, depending upon the strength of the bear market in progress.

The best period to buy stocks is when this indicator drops to below 30 percent. The best period for taking profits is when the percentage is above 70 percent.

PRICE/EARNINGS RATIO OF THE DJIA

The price per earnings (P/E) ratio of the Dow Jones Industrial Average is based on 12-month earnings figures for the component companies of the DJIA. This figure is reported in Barron's each week on the market laboratory page. In the past 25 years, the P/E ratio has fluctuated between 10 P/E and 18 P/E. When the P/E is below 10, market prices are relatively cheap, and the market is near a bottom. When the P/E ratio is 18 or above, market prices are relatively expensive, and the market is near a top.

For example, the market reached a peak in 1961 with a P/E of 24, in 1966 with a P/E of 18, in 1968 with a P/E of 18, in 1971 with a P/E of 18, and in 1983 with a P/E of 30. The market reached a bottom in 1970 with a P/E of 11, in 1974 with a P/E of 6, in 1978 with a P/E of 7, in 1980 with a P/E of 6.5, and in 1982 with a P/E of 8.5.

DIVIDEND YIELD OF THE DJIA

The dividend yield of the DJIA is based on 12-month dividends for its component companies. This indicator is similar in its behavior to the price/earnings ratio of the DJIA. This indicator is also known as the "dividend cost indicator"; the price you pay for $1 of dividends. Near the top of bull markets, the dividend cost indicator exceeded 30. This means that, near market tops (if you own a portfolio composed of Dow Industrial stocks), for every $1 of dividends received, you pay $30. When this takes place, the dividend yield on the Dow Jones Industrial Average is an unattractive 3.3 percent. The probability that prices will continue to rise when the dividend yield for the Dow Jones Industrial Average is under 3.3 percent, is very small. This indicates that stock prices are too high, and that a price correlation of about 10 to 15 percent will follow.

At the end of 1985, the dividend yield for the Dow Jones Industrial Average Stock was as follows:

Alcoa	3.1
Allied Corporation	3.8
American Can	4.8
American Express	2.6
AT&T	4.8
Bethlehem Steel	0.0
Chevron	6.4
DuPont	4.5
Eastman Kodak	4.3
Exxon	6.5
General Electric	3.2
General Motors	7.0
Goodyear	5.2
Int'l Harvester	0
IBM	2.9
Inco	1.5
Int'l Paper	4.8
McDonald's	1.1
Merck	2.6
MMM	4.0
Owens Illinois	3.4
Philip Morris	4.5
Procter & Gamble	3.7
Sears	4.6
Texaco	9.7*
Union Carbide	4.5
United Technologies	3.1
U.S. Steel	4.5
Westinghouse	2.7
Woolworth	3.4
Average Yield:	3.7

Near market bottoms, the dividend yield exceeds 6 percent. For example, in 1974, near the market bottom, the dividend yield was 6.2 percent; in 1982, near the market bottom, the dividend yield was 6.8 percent.

---

*The 9.7 percent dividend yield on Texaco was high due to the litigation of Penzoil at that time. Excluding Texaco, the average dividend yield was 3.7 percent.

PUT/CALL RATIO (ON THE CBOE)

This indicator compares the volume of put options to call options on the Chicago Board Options Exchange (CBOE). When put options trading activity increases in comparison to call options trading activity, this ratio rises reflecting an increase in the pessimism of traders. When put options trading activity declines in comparison to call options activity, this ratio drops. When this ratio rises to 0.70 - 0.80 on a five-day average basis, it indicates that the market is oversold (a relatively high level of pessimism) and the market is ready for a technical rally. When this indicator drops to below 0.40 it indicates a relatively high level of optimism and that a market downside correction is approaching.

SEAT PRICE (NYSE)

The rise and fall of seat prices on the NYSE generally follow the market. For example, in 1982 near the market bottom, a seat on the NYSE was sold for $190,000. One year later, near the 1983 market top, seats were sold for $400,000 each.

SENTIMENT INDEX OF LEADING
ADVISORY SERVICES

This index is based on Investor Intelligence's weekly survey of the percentage of Advisory Services that are bullish and bearish.

When the percentage of advisory services who are bullish exceeds 60 percent, it indicates that the market is reaching a peak that will be followed by a market decline. When the percentage of advisory services who are bullish declines to 30 percent, it indicates that the market is near a trough that will be followed by a market advance.

Advisory Services are for the most part trend-followers. More and more services turn bullish as the Dow-Jones Industrial Average advances, and, conversely, more and more turn bearish as the average declines. As a result, they are right as the trend progresses in the same direction and wrong just before the trend is ready to reverse. Whenever the Advisory Services reach a peak of bullishness, the market falls; whenever they reach a trough of bullishness, the market advances.

The sentiment index is measured by dividing the percentage of services reported as bullish by the sum of bullish and bearish percentages.

Peaks of Bullish Sentiment were reached in January 1966 (88%), October 1967 (68%), December 1968 (64%), November 1969 (58%), March 1971 (82%), December 1972 (82%), October 1973 (66%), February 1975 (74%), February 1976 (90%), January 1977 (80%), and August 1978 (74%). All peaks were followed by market declines. Troughs of bullish sentiment were reached in November 1966 (32%), April 1968 (16%), August 1969 (26%), May 1970 (32%), December 1971 (52%), June 1972 (42%), and July 1974 (30%). All the troughs were followed by market advances.

NYSE MEMBERS' SHORT SELLING RATIO

Members of the New York Stock Exchange tend to be correct in their selling short activities, primarily because of their professional know-how and experience. On the other hand, public investors tend to be wrong in their selling short activities for two basic reasons: (1) they react emotionally to daily updates from the media, and (2) they lack professional insight.

A downward correction is usually signaled when NYSE members account for 85 percent of all short sales, while nonmember short selling is less than 1 percent of total weekly volume. A strongly bullish reading would find NYSE members accounting for less than 65 percent of total short sales, with nonmembers showing 3 percent or more of total weekly volume.

THE SPECIALIST SHORT RATIO

This indicator describes the selling short activity of specialists whose function and responsibility on the floor of the New York Stock Exchange is to help maintain a fair and orderly market in specific securities.

It is the ratio of the number of shares sold short by specialists as a percentage of the total round lot shares sold short on the New York Stock Exchange. It is calculated and published weekly in several trade journals, with a two-week lag in reporting the data.

A ratio of near 50 percent describes average short selling activity of the specialists on the floor of the New York Stock Exchange. A ratio of over 63 percent indicates an increase in specialists' pessimism, which usually takes place when the market is near a top. For example, this happened in April 1959, June 1960, March 1961, November 1961, March 1962, March 1965, March 1966, February 1967, May 1968, and September 1971.

A ratio below 40 percent indicates an increase in specialists' optimism, which usually takes place when the market is near a bottom. For example, this happened in September 1953, January 1958, October 1962, August 1970, and October 1974.

A lower specialist short sale ratio is bullish. A higher specialist short sale is bearish.

ODD-LOT SHORT SALE RATIO

An odd lot transaction is a trade of less than 100 shares. It is usually used by small investors who do not have enough capital to trade in lots of 100 shares. A short sale is carried out in anticipation of a decline in the price of the stock.

The odd-lot short sale ratio is calculated by dividing the daily odd-lot short sales to total odd lot sales. It is a daily percentage ratio. A 10-day moving average could also be used to smooth the daily fluctuations. When the odd-lot short sales ratio approaches 6 percent, it indicates that a major market bottom has developed. When it approaches ½ percent, it indicates that a market top has developed.

The hypothesis is that odd-lotters (small investors) are the most consistently inaccurate investors, especially in major market turning points. An increase in the odd-lot short ratio indicates an increase in public pessimism. It usually takes place near market bottoms. This is exactly where you want to buy. A decline in the odd-lot short sales ratio indicates an increase in optimism (public optimism), and this is the time when you should sell.

NYSE SHORT INTEREST RATIO

The short interest is the total of all short positions expressed in shares. This total is reported on the 15th of each month and is released on the 20th of each month. The NYSE short interest ratio is the monthly ratio of the short interest to the average NYSE daily volume. An increase in this ratio indicates an increase in the short interest. This increase is considered to be a bullish development because short positions eventually have to be covered, thus creating a potential demand for stocks.

STANDARD & POOR'S LOW-PRICED INDEX

This index measures the activity of speculative stocks. It is based on monthly figures that are calculated by averaging weekly closings of this index.

THE SHORT-TERM TRADING INDEX (TRIN)

What is TRIN and how can I use it?

The Short-Term Trading Index is the ratio of the advance/decline issues ratio to the upside/downside volume ratio. It compares the number of declining and advancing issues to the volume of advancing and declining issues.

This index appears on quote machines as TRIN or STKS or MKDS (TRIN on the Quotron machine). It describes at any moment during trading hours — and at the close of the trading day — the relative behavior of the volume against the relative behavior of the issues. For example, at the end of a trading day, there were 900 advancing issues and 450 declining issues. The advancing issues exceeded the declining issues by a ratio of 2:1. On the same day, the volume occurring in the advancing issues was 48 million shares and the volume occurring in the declining issues as 12 million shares, a ratio of 4:1. The TRIN at the market close on that day would be: Issues Ratio equals 2:1 divided by Volume Ratio equals 4:1. The TRIN is equal to 2:4 or 0.50.

Since this is rather complicated, the following formula is presented.

$$TRIN = \frac{I}{V}$$

$$I = \frac{\text{Number of advancing issues}}{\text{Number of declining issues}}$$

$$V = \frac{\text{Upside volume (volume in advancing issues)}}{\text{Downside volume (volume in declining issues)}}$$

When the trading index is equal to 0.50, it indicates that the daily volume on the New York Stock Exchange is twice as strong as the number of issues traded on that same day.

A reading of .75 or lower for a 10-day average, together with a one-day reading of .75 or lower, indicates an overbought market, or a good time to sell stocks. When the 10-day TRIN exceeds 1.25 and the one-day TRIN is below 0.50, it indicates an oversold market condition, or a good time to buy stocks.

The trading index as an indicator will give different signals if you look ahead one week, one month, or three months. The percentage return on your investment will vary depending on the level of the indicator.

CASE IN POINT: In June of 1982, the market was oversold. The 10-day TRIN readings for the week starting May 30 were as follows:

1982	May 30	June 1	June 2	June 3	June 4
TRIN					
10-day	closed	1.31	1.23	1.20	1.28
D.J.I.A.	closed	814.97	816.88	816.50	804.98

About one year later, in June of 1983, the market was overbought. The 10-day TRIN readings were as follows:

1983	June 20	June 21	June 22	June 23	June 24
TRIN					
10-day	0.83	0.77	0.77	0.79	0.77
D.J.I.A.	1239.18	1247.40	1245.69	1241.79	1241.69

The Dow Jones Industrial average rose within about one year from the 810 level to the 1245 level — an increase of 435 points or 53.7 percent. The TRIN 10-day index changed from an oversold 1.25 level to an overbought 0.79 level.

THE UTILITIES INDEX

Utilities are often bought by conservative investors seeking above-average dividend income and relative safety of principal. Prices of utilities' stocks are sensitive to the outlook for interest rates. When interest rates go down, the dividend yield from utilities becomes more attractive. For that reason, the Utilities Index has been a reliable leading indicator for forecasting trends of interest rates. The Dow Jones Utility Average often makes its bottoms and tops before the Dow Jones Industrial Average.

VOLUME CUMULATIVE (UPSIDE—DOWNSIDE)

Each day the net change in volume is calculated by subtracting the downside volume on the New York Stock Exchange from the upside volume. This net change is then added to the previous day's cumulative. The behavior of the cumulative is then compared to the behavior of the Dow Jones Industrial Average. This is a leading market indicator. It often reaches a new high before the Dow will start an upside move.

VOLUME ASE/NYSE AND OTC/NYSE RATIOS

One of the methods of identifying excessive speculation is to compare the volume on the American Stock Exchange and the volume of Over-the-Counter trading with the volume on the New York Stock Exchange.

ASE/NYSE and OTC/NYSE volume ratios are measures of the speculative activity of the public. Stocks listed on the American Stock Exchange usually represent smaller companies and are thus more speculative. Near market bottoms these ratios decline, indicating the lack of the public's speculative activity. Near market tops these ratios increase, indicating excessive public speculation.

In recent years, some of the speculative activity has moved from stocks listed on the American Stock Exchange to the listed option market, where the public can speculate by buying call or put options with a relatively low capital investment.

YIELD GAP (S&P STOCK YIELD VS. BOND YIELD)

This is the spread between yields of the S&P400 industrial stocks and the AAA corporate bonds. For example, when the yield on stocks is 5 percent, and the yield on bonds is 11 percent, the spread (gap) is -6 percent. An increase in the spread occurs when the yield on bonds rises and the yield on stocks declines or when the yield on bonds declines less than the decline in the yields on stocks. A higher gap indicates that your return from bonds is more attractive, while a lower gap indicates that your return from stocks is more favorable. When the gap reaches a level of about -7 percent, it signals that the stock market is near a top and could be vulnerable to a major decline in prices.

MOVING AVERAGES

The use of moving averages in technical analysis is very popular. It is important to distinguish between a simple average and a moving average. A simple average is calculated by dividing the sum of two or more quantities (in technical analysis usually price or volume data) by the number of data. For example, the average weekly volume is calculated by adding the daily volume and dividing by 5 (five trading days in one week).

A moving average is calculated in a continuous manner. The new information is added and the oldest information is subtracted each time the average is calculated. For example, a five-day moving average of volume data is calculated each day by adding the latest day volume and subtracting the oldest day volume, and then dividing by 5. It is updated continuously. It is popular because it is easy to calculate with a computer. It is also sensitive to recent changes. Many professionals use a 200-day moving average to identify price and volume trends.

A COMPOSITE INDEX OF SEVERAL INDICATORS

Since the accuracy of the market timing indicators described in this chapter will vary from time to time and from market to market, many professionals do not depend on one indicator to make their investment decisions. Rather, they use a combination of indicators. For example, it is possible that at any time, an analysis of indicators will show that seven are positive (bullish) and three are negative (bearish).

One example of a composite indicator is the "Wall Street Week Index" (originated by Robert Neurock), a show which is presented weekly on public television. When the index is equal to zero, it means that the number of positive indicators is equal to the number of negative indicators. When the index is equal to -3, it means that the number of negative technical indicators exceeds the number of positive indicators by 3.

ANALYSIS OF TIMING INDICATORS

How can I tell if a timing indicator is useful and accurate?

The analysis of a timing indicator involves the study of its past behavior over a period of time. This analysis helps to assign probabilities to the possible direction and level of future prices within a specific period of time. The analysis will determine if a timing indicator can help you identify market tops or bottoms.

The concept of timing indicators is not unique to the field of investments. Economists for many years have used various indicators (leading, coincidential, lagging) to predict the future course of the economy. It is important to note that the level of indicators, under extreme market bottom and top conditions, may have secular trends over a period of years. It is related to changes in interest rates level, price per earnings ratios, and changes in the investor's psychology.

The analysis of timing indicators is based on common principles of scientific inquiry involving four stages:

1. Observation: The collection of historical data and facts.
2. Hypothesis: The development of a theory and making of assumptions regarding the data collected in stage 1. It also involves the statement of "hunches" as to the patterns in the data.
3. Predictions: Do the data suggest that there is any predictive value for the anticipation of behavior of the data?
4. Verification: Can the theory be substantiated and can certain conclusions be determined?

HOW TO USE TIMING INDICATORS

Each timing indicator, at a specific level, will generate neutral, bullish, or bearish signals. The indicators (one or several) are used to identify market bottom and top conditions, to help in making buy and sell decisions, and are used also to identify trends in the market.

Specific securities and the securities market fluctuate continuously. Often these fluctuations are random, with no specific identifiable cause. Sometimes prices do change because of specific nonrandom reasons.

The concept of separation between random and nonrandom moves was introduced about 100 years ago in the field of production and manufacturing control. It was based on statistical probability theory. In the field of engineering, it became an accepted practice to specify each important quality characteristic of a given product by quality limits within which a product is acceptable. A defective part is one whose quality characteristics fall outside the specified range. Control limits have been developed by industry for the purpose of attaining economic control of quality of product in mass production.

The same concept can be applied to the use of stock market timing indicators to separate between random and nonrandom moves in stock prices. When an indicator reaches the control limit (based on past experience), the hypothesis is that a new condition based on "a new cause" exists.

TECHNICAL ANALYSIS

Charts

How can technical charts help me?

Charts are used as a tool in trend analysis. They provide a history of prices in compact graphic form and enable the investor to evaluate his or her performance. Some commonly used charts show daily high, low, and closing prices as well as daily volume.

Other charts known as Point and Figure charts show price changes in a security independently of time. In a Point and Figure chart, successive upward price changes are plotted with an X on the same vertical line, and when a price reversal takes place, successive downward prices are plotted with an O on a new vertical line. This process repeats itself with each succeeding upward or downward price movement. This type of chart often produces a clear picture of trends. The following Point and Figure chart describes changes in gold prices from January 1, 1982 to January 1, 1986.

Sample Point and Figure Chart
LONDON GOLD PRICE 1/1/82 — 1/1/86

LONDON GOLD P.M. FIXING ONLY

(1/1/82 - present)

LONDON GOLD
THE CHART SHOWS A BUY SIGNAL AT 328. THE FIRST NEW SIGNAL SINCE THE 5/83 SELL. UPSIDE PRICE OBJECTIVE IS 420. REVERSAL AT 312.

Technical charts can demonstrate if the current price is high or low based on an historical basis. They can also bring to the investor's attention unusual price and volume behavior in a particular stock.

Charts can also be used to identify the price range in which a particular stock is being accumulated or distributed.

Charts are constructed to show the past record of price and volume fluctuations daily, weekly, or monthly. They are used as a tool to recognize patterns of movements and trends. The most common chart patterns that the technical analyst looks for are:

Uptrend, downtrend, and sideways trendline channels

Upcurve and downcurve trendlines

Upside and downside climax

Support and resistance zones

Head and shoulders formations

Double tops and bottoms formations

Long base and volume developments

Breakouts

Ascending and descending triangles

Up and down flags

One- and two-day reversals

Breakaway, runaway, and exhaustion gaps

Chartists and tape readers believe that "the tape tells all." In other words, there is no need to spend time and effort analyzing the fundamentals of the company. The analysis and the interpretation of chart formations is their secret to successful investing.

Human Emotions

Technical analysis is based on the observation that stock prices go up or down, not only in reaction to changing fundamental business conditions such as earnings and dividends or changes in the economic outlook, but prices also fluctuate in response to warm, human emotions rather than the analysis of cold facts. Emotions such as fear, overconfidence, greed, and crowd psychology often play an important role in individual investors' decisions. Technical analysis attempts to identify these conditions.

Technical Alerts

What is a "technical" alert signal?

An **alert signal** is a warning to the investor that unusual (statistically nonrandom) behavior is occurring in the stock. This warning signal may affect the investor's decision to buy, hold, or sell.

A **price alert** is an unusual price behavior. For example, a stock might break through a moving average on the downside or the upside. The stock might also break through the highest or the lowest price of the last 75 trading days. This also indicates an unusual price change for the day, week, or month.

A **trend alert** is a signal or warning to alert the investor when a trend is changing to or from an upward, downward, or neutral trend position.

A **volume alert** is an unusual volume behavior that alerts the investor to changes in supply of or demand for a stock. This becomes apparent when high volume occurs on either the downside or the upside. An unusual behavior might be a sudden fivefold increase in a daily volume as compared with the average daily volume for the last six months.

What is the technical definition of a market consolidation?

When prices go up within a major uptrend, short-term fluctuations may give false alert signals in reaction to a pullback. When prices retreat on light volume, often the market consolidates but the major trend remains intact.

MARKET BOTTOM AND TOP CONDITIONS

The indicators described in this chapter, with the help of technical analysis, are used to identify market bottoms (support levels) and market tops (resistance levels). Usually a composite of several timing indicators is used.

Near bottom conditions (support levels) you can expect several indicators to reach extreme conditions (based on historical observations). For example, the price per earnings ratio of the Dow Jones Industrial Average is below 8. The number of advisory services bullish is below 30 percent. Four months have passed without the stock of General Motors making a new low. The ratio of insiders selling to insiders buying is below 0.5. Mutual funds cash position is above 12 percent. There is a substantial increase in volume after a long decline. Although under different market conditions the extreme level of the indicators may vary, a composite or a combination of the indicators will signal a change in market direction.

Near market top conditions (resistance levels) you can expect the timing indicators to reach extreme levels. For example, the price per earnings ratio of the Dow Jones Industrial Average could reach 15 or higher. The number of advisory services bullish could exceed 80 percent. Four months have passed without General Motors making a new high. The ratio of insiders selling to insiders buying could exceed 2.5. Mutual funds cash position could decline to below 7 percent.

It is unwise to depend on one particular indicator because no indicator is perfect. However, a review of a number of indicators could benefit you considerably by improving your investment performance.

You should be bullish only when several indicators simultaneously give bullish signals. Similarly, you should be bearish only when several indicators simultaneously show bearish signals. You don't necessarily have to buy and sell every day. When the majority of the indicators are neutral, the market may fluctuate at random. When this happens, you should reduce your trading activity and concentrate only on special situations.

CASE IN POINT: On June 21, 1981 the Dow Jones Industrial Average closed at 1006.66. The majority of investment advisors, portfolio managers, and individual investors were overoptimistic. The Trading Index (TRIN) reached 0.54 on that day, the three-day TRIN was 0.79, and the ten-day TRIN was 0.89. For the week ending June 21, 1981, the net cumulative volume was a positive 59,598,000 shares on the upside. The consensus was bullish.

However, mass psychology can change rapidly. One year later on June 18, 1982, Dow Jones closed at 788.62, a decline of 218 points, or about 22 percent since 1981.

The market was in the process of developing a bottom during June of 1982. This was reflected by the following indicators:

- The net cumulative volume for the week ending June 18, 1982 was a negative 80,810,000 on the downside.
- The one-day TRIN reached a high of 1.44 on June 19, 1982, and the ten-day TRIN hit an oversold level of 1.34, indicating panic selling.
- The sentiment index of leading advisory services showed on June 11, 1982 that the percentage of advisors who are bearish rose to a high level of 57.6 percent.
- The specialist short ratio declined to a low of 28.2 percent.
- The percentage of the New York Stock Exchange stocks above their 10-week moving average hit a low of 17.4 percent as

of June 16, 1982 (when the Dow Industrials reached 796.90).

- The volume of trading on the American Stock exchange declined to about 8 percent of the New York Stock Exchange volume, indicating the absence of speculative activity.

- Institutional cash reserves rose sharply to 14.3 percent of net assets.

- The prime bank loan rate stood at 16.5 percent, 90-day CDs were yielding 15 percent, and long-term municipal bonds were yielding over 12 percent.

During that same week, Dow Industrials was down by 3.69 percent, Dow Utilities declined by 2.73 percent, Dow Transportation was down by 3.88 percent, the American Stock Exchange Index was down by 5.33 percent, and the S&P 500 was down by 3.65 percent. The decline was across the board.

The consensus was overly pessimistic — precisely why this was the right time to buy stocks. The downside risk was small but the upside potential was substantial. The risk/reward ratio was favorable with an upside potential of 500 points versus a downside risk of 50 points.

You run the risk of missing a bottom and also a good part of the early stages of the upmove if you decide to wait and postpone the purchase of stocks until it is clear to everyone that the market did in fact hit the final bottom and a new major bull market is in progress. It is important that you master the necessary self-discipline and not try to buy exactly at the bottom and sell exactly at the top.

THE PRICE OF A STOCK VERSUS
THE VALUE OF A COMPANY

**What is the difference between the price of the
stock and the value of the company?**

It is important to understand the difference between
a stock traded in an open public market and the company
with its assets, liabilities, earnings and losses. The price of
a stock may go up or down during a period when the
company's fundamentals remain unchanged. When you
buy the whole company, your criteria for investment are
based on a different set of requirements from when you buy
1,000 or 10,000 shares of common stock. When you buy a
stock, you buy a price — a price that will fluctuate. Every
stock has its own price behavior characteristics. Behind
every stock is a different group of investors buying or
selling it.

CHAPTER 6

Fundamental Analysis

What is fundamental analysis?

Fundamental analysis attempts to determine the underlying "value" of a corporation. This includes the analysis of its balance sheet (assets and liabilities) and profit-and-loss statement, book value per share, earnings per share, cash flow per share, and dividends per share. It attempts to evaluate the effectiveness of research and development, the introduction of new products, and the company's competitive edge. Fundamental analysis is extremely important for long-range investment decisions. It carries less weight in short-term trading decisions. Fundamental analysis may apply to one corporation, one industry, or the market as a whole.

What are the objectives of fundamental analysis?

The purpose is to determine if the market price of the stock is undervalued or overvalued. Fundamental analysis attempts to answer the following questions: Is the stock selling below book value? Is the stock selling at a low multiple of price to earnings? Is the stock selling at a low multiple of price to cash flow? Is the stock selling at a relatively attractive dividend yield?

Historical trends of fundamental information are analyzed to help in making future projections. Fundamental analysis is specifically important in evaluating the downside risk potential of a particular stock or of the market as a whole.

BALANCE SHEET ANALYSIS

The analysis of a balance sheet is a key factor in fundamental analysis. Determining the value of the company's assets and comparing the assets to the company's liabilities require understanding of acceptable accounting procedures. The stated accounting value of the assets could be higher or lower than their actual liquidation value. You must also understand that a balance sheet is a picture of the financial condition of the company on one specific day only. This condition could change from one day to another. For example, a company may show $1 million cash in the bank on December 31, yet on January 2, the balance may decline to $0.

The analysis of a company's liabilities could also be quite complicated. For example, a lease obligation could be a liability if the company has to continue to pay the rent and not utilize the space. Yet in some cases a long-term lease could be a major asset when the rents go up and the company can sell the lease. Lease obligations are not listed on the balance sheet. Yet they could be either an asset or a liability, depending on the circumstance.

Many investors fail to understand that when you buy a stock in a company you really buy a piece of its balance sheet.

BOOK VALUE PER SHARE (NET WORTH)

Book value per share is a measure of shareholders' equity in the corporation. It includes both tangible (such as equipment, inventories, and receivables) and intangibles. The book value per share is calculated by taking the total assets and subtracting the total liabilities (such as accounts payable, taxes, and long-term debt) and dividing this difference by the number of shares outstanding.

How is book value per share used in fundamental analysis?

Book value per share is compared to the price per share in the open market. When the book value per share is below the price per share, the stock is considered undervalued.

EARNINGS PER SHARE

Corporate earnings (as reported to stockholders) cover past information such as last fiscal year or last quarter. However, per-share earnings forecasts are more important. Earnings estimates for the next four quarters and year-to-year percentage change are more relevant in making investment decisions than past or current earnings.

For companies with convertible bonds, preferred stocks, or warrants outstanding, the convertible securities must be assumed converted in calculations of earnings per share "fully diluted." Earnings per share calculated on a "fully diluted" basis are lower than the regular calculation of earnings per share on actual current number of shares outstanding. However, "fully diluted" earnings per share reflect more accurately the long-term earnings power of the company.

CASH FLOW PER SHARE

Cash flow is the sum of net income plus depreciation and depletion charges. Cash flow is a measure of "sources of funds" from operations. "Cash flow" per share is "net income before depreciation" per share plus "depreciation and depletion charges" per share.

Why is cash flow per share an important measure of corporate profitability?

"Cash flow" per share is a superior measure of corporate profitability. It eliminates the distortion of earnings per share resulting from different depreciation methods. It is an indicator of the company's "internal cash generating ability." Often this is a more accurate measure of corporate profitability than "earnings per share".

Depreciation in dollars is the amount that assets are written off in a single year. It is a noncash charge (but tax deductible) against earnings.

SALES PER SHARE

An uptrend in sales per share often suggests an improved outlook of earnings per share. When sales per share decline together with earnings per share, this would be a negative sign.

DIVIDEND YIELD

How is the current dividend yield on a stock calculated?

You divide the annual dividend paid by the company to shareholders by the current market price of the stock.

However, you should remember that a dividend is declared by the company's board of directors, who may maintain, raise, cut, or suspend the dividend. A company does not have to pay a dividend to its common shareholders. Growth stocks usually pay only a small portion of their earnings in dividends. Mature companies pay to shareholders a higher portion of their earnings.

NET CURRENT ASSETS (NET WORKING CAPITAL)

Net current assets is calculated by subtracting current liabilities from current assets. It is also known as "net working capital."

It indicates the corporation's ability to pay its current debt obligations.

CURRENT RATIO

This is the ratio of current assets to current liabilities. "Current" means less than one year. For example, a liability due in less than one year is considered current. Similarly, an account receivable due in less than one year is considered a current asset. It is a measure of corporate liquidity.

A ratio of over 2.5 to 1 is financially sound. A ratio of less than 1 to 1 indicates that the company may have difficulty paying its short-term debts.

DEBT-TO-EQUITY RATIO

This ratio measures the outstanding debt of the corporation relative to the common shareholders' equity base. It describes the company's financial structure. When a company has no debt, the ratio is equal to zero. When the debt-to-equity ratio rises above 50 percent, the financial structure is subject to greater risks. It may be difficult for the company to borrow additional funds. Also, the interest cost of carrying the high debt could adversely affect profitability.

RETURN ON STOCKHOLDERS' EQUITY

This measures the profitability of a business in terms of net income divided by stockholders' equity. This is a "bottom-line" figure describing the financial health of a corporation.

The return on shareholders' equity is the result of two other important ratios — profit margin and equity turnover. Profit margin is the ratio of net income to sales. Equity turnover is the ratio of sales to shareholders' equity.

You can calculate the return on shareholders' equity by multiplying the profit margin ratio by the equity turnover ratio.

BONDS VERSUS STOCKS

What is the difference between owning a bond and a stock?

As an owner of a stock you own a piece of the company. Should the company do well, the value of the ownership will in time go up. Should the company's earnings deteriorate, the value of your ownership will in turn probably also decline.

When you own a bond, you do not own a piece of the company. Instead, you are a creditor to the company. You are entitled to receive interest, usually at a fixed rate, but the value of your bond will not change as the value of the company changes. You do not share in the increase of the company's profits or common stock dividend payouts. Nor will you suffer to the same extent as the owner of a stock when earnings deteriorate.

When you buy a bond, you should analyze its safety and its ability to pay the interest. For that reason, the rating of bonds is most important. When you buy a stock, you should analyze its potential earnings and its ability to increase its shareholders' equity value and its cash dividends.

How should I choose between bonds and stocks?

You compare interest yields with the dividend yield available on common stocks. For example, when the interest yield on a bond is 12 percent and the dividend yield on a stock is 4 percent, the yield difference is 8 percent (12 percent minus 4 percent). This difference of 8 percent is in favor of the bond. However, during periods of inflation bond prices often decline. Therefore, you should compare the expected total return (yield plus capital appreciation) from a stock to that of a bond.

How should I select stocks for my portfolio?

It depends on your personal needs and objectives. Generally, you should follow the rules described in the chapter on Investment Philosophy. Evaluate the relative risks in relation to the potential rewards. Compare the price of the stock to its book value. Compare the stock cash dividend yield to other available rates of return from corporate bonds and Treasury securities. Study the past performance of management.

VALUE ANALYSIS

Stocks sometimes sell way above their liquidation value due to overoptimism or overexpectation. Sometimes they sell way below their liquidation value due to over-pessimism and depressed overall market conditions. From time to time stocks in a particular industry could be out of favor and sell at bargain prices.

The objective of "value analysis" is to determine, using various financial ratios, if the market price of the stock is too high or too low — is the stock undervalued or overvalued?

UNDERVALUED SITUATIONS

Stocks are undervalued when they sell at a fraction of their liquidation value. As a prudent investor, you should search for companies selling for a small fraction of their true worth.

How can I tell when a stock is "undervalued"?

A stock is considered undervalued when it is selling in the open market below its "intrinsic value." This will happen when the market price is below the liquidation value of its assets. Undervalued stocks should meet one or more of the following conditions:

- Stocks selling below their book value
- Stocks selling at a low multiple of price to earnings (usually less than 10 to 1)
- Stocks selling at a low multiple of price to cash flow per share (usually less than 5 to 1)
- Stocks paying a relatively high dividend

In the case where the company's assets might be liquidated, the liquidation value should exceed the market price of the stock.

Why should I buy an undervalued stock?

When the market price of a stock is below its intrinsic value, in most cases either the stock market will recognize its value and the stock will subsequently go up in price, or its assets will be acquired by another corporation. In any event, the patient investor should benefit.

SPECIAL SITUATIONS

A stock is considered a special situation if there are one or more reasons to purchase the stock. For example:

- It may be a possible takeover, a merger, or an acquisition candidate.
- An industry or a group may be temporarily oversold. This would represent a special buying opportunity.
- There could be a sharp improvement in the earnings outlook.

When you find a special situation, the profit potential should far exceed the investment risks involved.

ACQUISITIONS AND MERGERS CANDIDATES

The urge to "acquire and merge" is an important characteristic in the American business scene. Many companies have discovered that it is easier to expand their businesses by buying a long established business, which was developed by someone else's hard work, rather than building through internal growth. An investor buying the stock of a company that might be acquired often expects its price to appreciate within a relatively short period of time.

Many large American companies grew through external growth by acquiring other well-established public companies. For example:

- Gulf + Western has four operating segments: Entertainment (Paramount Pictures, Madison Square Garden); Publishing (Simon & Schuster, Prentice-Hall); Consumer and Industrial Products (Kayser-Roth, Simmon Bedding, A.P.S. auto parts); and Financial Services (Associates Corp.).
- ITT's operations include telecommunication equipment and services, aerospace electronics, industrial automotive, Sheraton Hotels, Hartford Insurance, international telex, and ITT long-distance telephone service.
- IC Industries is a holding company which owns the Illinois Central Gulf Railroad, Abex Corporation, Pepsi-Cola General Bottlers, Midas International (auto replacement services), Pet Inc. (food products), Hussman (refrigeration equipment), and Pneumo Corp. (aerospace).
- Kidde is a diversified manufacturer whose holdings include Fenwall and Kidde Fire Protection Equipment, Globe Security Guards, Jacuzzi Auto Parts, Nissen and Universal Gyms, and PGA Golf Equipment.
- Loews which operates movie theaters and hotels acquired Lorillard Corp., producer of Kent, Newport, and True cigarettes; and owns interest in CNA Financial and Bulova Watch.

All of these successful and diversified companies grew through good, external acquisitions.

ECONOMIC OUTLOOK ANALYSIS

The average range of long-term growth rate of the U.S. economy, as measured by the Gross National Product (GNP), has fluctuated between 3 percent and 7 percent.

(The dollar value of the total annual output of final goods and services in the nation is its gross national product.) However, business activity has been experiencing short-term fluctuation of boom and bust, business cycles, recession, inflation, and unemployment. Many theories, none of them entirely satisfactory, have been advanced to explain the cycles of bad and good times. In fact, there have been numerous recessions (periods of contraction of economic activity): 1904, 1907, 1914, 1921, 1930 (The Great Depression), 1949, 1958, 1962, 1974, and 1981.

Federal Reserve intervention, through monetary policy, greatly affects the outlook for interest rates, the bond market, and the stock market. The objective of monetary policy is to foster sustained economic growth and employment in a context of reasonable price stability.

Once you predict a specific economic outlook, your investment strategy will change. For example, if you assume that the inflation rate will accelerate, you should invest in inflation-hedge stocks. If you assume that the economy will go through a period of deflation, you should invest in bonds. If you assume that the economy is entering an up cycle, you should buy cyclical stocks. If you anticipate a recession, you should be defensive. If interest rates are expected to decline, your bond portfolio will do very well. But if interest rates are expected to rise, you could suffer substantial losses.

CASE IN POINT: The recession that began in July of 1981 ended in July 1982, when the administration reduced the personal income tax by $33 billion and by increased social security benefits by $12 billion. This brought about an increase in consumer spending. From August to December 1981, the prime bank loan rate was cut in several steps (12 times) from 20.5 percent to 15.75 percent.

As the economy improves, business activity and corporate profits rise. The stock market, in anticipation of these changes in economic trends, will often start rising about six months before the economy starts to recover.

FUNDAMENTAL ANALYSIS VERSUS TECHNICAL ANALYSIS

What is the difference between fundamental analysis and technical analysis?

You should distinguish between the company's performance (sales, earnings, assets) and the stock performance (price of the stock in the open market). Fundamental analysis investigates the company and its financial statements. Technical analysis attempts to predict the future behavior of the stock in the marketplace. Technical analysis evaluates price and volume movements and various charts and timing indicators.

CHAPTER 7

Investment Advisors and Mutual Funds

SELECTING AN INVESTMENT ADVISOR

Most people don't have the time, the information, the knowledge, the inclination, or the patience to manage their own investments. Successful investing is a full-time job. It requires many resources that are not available to most people.

According to the Securities and Exchange Commission, there were 10,908 investment advisors registered as of Sept. 30, 1985, up from 9,083 a year earlier.

There are so many advisors available. How can I choose the right one for me?

Investment advisory and management firms provide a range of services and have varying investment philosophies. They vary in size from one-man firms to organizations with several thousand employees.

Investment advisory firms cannot be all things to all people. Each firm has its own specialty. Some firms specialize in commodities, others in bonds or equities. Several advisors specialize in writing option strategies, others in buying securities that are undervalued. Some are short-term traders, others buy for long-term appreciation.

You should select the one that will work hard for you. Define your specific needs. Look for the advisor who will give you personal service and individual attention, someone who will help you attain your specific objectives. It is important that you select an advisor (a personal one or a mutual fund management organization) with whom you feel comfortable. Advice and counsel involve some hand-holding.

Don't hesitate to try a number of advisors until you find the right one for your needs. And don't feel you must limit yourself to one advisor. You may find you need to use several advisors to manage portions of your assets, each with varying areas of expertise.

Although most financial planners are highly qualified professionals who will help you develop a total financial plan to fit your own needs, you should be suspicious of anyone who may try to sell you his or her own products (such as insurance policies). Such products may not necessarily be for your best interests.

What kind of questions should I ask a prospective financial advisor?

Here are some of the most common questions that you should ask before deciding on a specific advisor:

1. What is the specific name and title of the individual within the organization who will be providing assistance? Will I be dealing directly with a qualified manager, or indirectly through his or her assistants?
2. Will the advisor be available to answer questions whenever needed?
3. How are the advisory fees determined? Are they based on time, asset value, or some other formula?

4. Can the advisory agreement be canceled at any time?
5. How much control will I have on the investment decisions? Is the account discretionary or nondiscretionary?
6. Will the advisor help to formulate long-range planning strategies?
7. What is the advisor's specialty — equities, bonds, mutual funds, municipalities, option writing, special situations, etc.?
8. What kind of clients make up the bulk of their business? Do they work primarily with individuals or corporations?
9. Does the advisor provide a monthly or quarterly statement of performance?

If I hire a money manager to handle my portfolio, what decisions will be made on my behalf?

The following decisions should be made by the manager based on the understanding of your investment needs and objectives:

1. Asset allocation decisions. What percentage of the portfolio should be invested in stocks? bonds? Treasury securities? cash? tax-free investments?
2. What to buy. The manager may select a specific stock, based on fundamental analysis such as earnings per share, book value, dividend yield, and so on.
3. When to buy. This decision is usually based on market timing indicators.
4. Which option to sell. This involves making decisions in regards to which expiration date and exercise price are to be selected.
5. When to sell either the stock (already owned) or an option (against the underlying security).
6. Whether to cover the option prior to expiration or let the option expire.
7. Selection of brokers for best execution of buy and sell orders.

It is very important for you, the investor, to determine exactly what your needs and objectives are, and to make sure that your advisor clearly understands them. These needs and objectives should be discussed, reviewed, analyzed, and adjusted periodically. Be sure that the both of you discuss and understand whether your investment account will be discretionary or nondiscretionary — that is, who will be responsible for the final investment decisions. Do you want your advisor to handle your account based on the needs you have outlined to him or her? Or do you want yourself to be responsible for having the "final" say? There can't be two captains on one ship. There can be only one manager of a portfolio if you want to have an effective, long-term financial relationship with your advisor.

DON'T BE A BACKSEAT DRIVER

How many times have you found yourself driving a car, only to discover that one of your passengers has decided it is his responsibility to help you? It's frustrating and almost never worthwhile to listen to a backseat driver — after all, the car can only be operated by one person. Financial investing works the same way. It's your money, and you want to get the most return possible on it. That's why you've selected an advisor to help you manage your money. After you select an investment advisor, it's your job to let go and let the advisor "do the driving."

"Backseat" investors generally fall into categories: either they don't trust their investor and feel compelled to "watchdog" every move, or they are overeager to be involved in every possible aspect of managing their portfolio. Either way, it's a lose-lose proposition for both the investor and the advisor. An overhelpful investor could be a nuisance, resulting only in irritating the advisor. Such a relationship could result in a deterioration of the services provided. The logical alternative in that case is to switch to another advisor. The advisor's desire to "do well" for a customer depends a lot on the customer's behavior. The bottom line is this: If you trust your advisor, leave him alone and let him do his job. If you don't like how your advisor works, find someone whom you do trust!

CASE IN POINT: Mrs. A.R. was an artist. She knew very little about investing. From time to time she read the *New York Times* and *Wall Street Journal*, always reacting to the latest news. In April of 1984, I recommended that she buy the common stock of CitiCorp (FNC). At the time, banks' stocks were under pressure due to negative publicity related to South American loans. Every time Mrs. R. read a negative article in the paper, she would call to remind me what a bad mistake I had made by recommending the purchase of this stock. About eight months later, in December, the stock was sold at 35½, without a loss or a gain to Mrs. R. Almost a year later, the common stock of CitiCorp reached a price of $46 a share, an increase of about 11 points or 33 percent. Her constant complaints did not result in any improvement, but brought about my request that she take her account somewhere else.

MUTUAL FUNDS

A mutual fund is a company that pools the money of many investors (its shareholders) to invest in a diversified portfolio of securities. Investments are made in stocks, bonds, money market instruments, options, or other securities to meet specific objectives. You pool your investment with those of like-minded investors who have common goals. You participate in the gains or losses experienced by the portfolio in which you invest.

All funds (no-load, low load, or load) charge a management fee for the management of the fund's portfolio. The prospectus of the fund contains a full disclosure on the fund's objectives, portfolio of securities, management purchase and redemption procedures, the costs, and the risks involved.

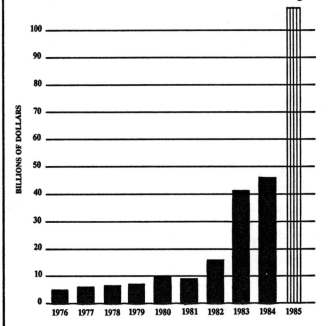

1985 Mutual Fund Sales Make History

Sales of stock, bond and income funds.

In 1985, mutual fund sales passed the $100 billion mark for the first time in the industry's history. This *more than doubled* the total record-breaking sales in 1984. The Investment Company Institute, the national association of the mutual fund industry, says that more than 22 million households or 25 percent of all American households now own mutual funds. Not only did 1985 sales reach an all-time high in the mutual funds which invest in the stock market, but this year witnessed the biggest surge in bond and income funds in the industry's 61 year history. These funds allow investors to participate in ownership of government-backed securities, morgage-backed securities, corporate bonds and tax-exempt municipal bonds. This tremendous growth brings the industry's total assets close to $500 billion. As recently as the beginning of the decade, mutual fund assets were only $95 billion.

Source: Investment Company Institute

In 1981, the net subscription to open-end mutual funds (subscription less redemptions — other than money market fund) was negative. More funds were redeemed than sold. By the end of 1982, net subscriptions of mutual funds rose about $800 million dollars. During 1983-1984 it averaged about $2 billion. In 1985 the buying of mutual funds rose sharply from the $2 billion rate to about $7 billion. Mutual funds have become more and more popular.

TABLE I

TOTAL SALES AND NET SALES OF MUTUAL FUNDS
(EXCLUDING MONEY MARKET AND
LIMITED MATURITY MUNICIPAL FUNDS)
(Billions of Dollars)

	Total Sales		Net Sales	
Type of Fund	1984	1985*	1984	1985*
Aggressive Growth	$ 5.1	$ 7.7	$ 1.9	$ 2.4
Growth	5.0	7.0	1.8	1.7
Growth & Income	6.4	9.3	3.0	4.6
Precious Metals	0.2	0.6	0.2	0.2
International	1.5	1.8	1.0	1.0
Total Equity	$18.2	$26.4	$ 7.9	$ 9.9
Balanced	0.2	0.5	(0.1)	0.2
Income	2.7	4.6	0.9	2.2
Option Income	1.9	2.9	1.6	2.2
U.S. Government Income	5.8	34.3	5.1	30.7
GNMA (Ginnie Mae)	2.9	12.7	2.4	11.2
Corporate Bond	4.3	9.5	2.5	7.1
Long-Term Municipal Bond	7.3	13.1	3.7	9.5
Single-State Muni. Bond	2.5	6.5	2.0	5.5
Total Bond & Income	$27.6	$84.1	$18.1	$68.6
Total, All Funds Excluding Money Market and Limited Maturity Municipal Funds	$45.8	$110.5	$26.0	$78.5

---

*Estimates for the full year 1985 are based on data for the first 11 months of this year.

TABLE II
ASSETS OF MUTUAL FUNDS*
(Billions of Dollars)

Type of Mutual Fund	Assets 1984	Assets 1985
Aggressive Growth	$ 16.8	$ 22.6
Growth	24.9	31.6
Growth & Income	31.8	42.5
Precious Metals	0.4	1.7
International	4.6	7.0
Total Equity	$ 78.5	$105.4
Balanced	$ 2.9	$ 3.6
Income	6.7	9.7
Option Income	3.4	5.5
U.S. Government Income	6.3	35.4
GNMA (Ginnie Mae)	4.0	16.4
Corporate Bond	14.5	22.8
Long-Term Municipal Bond	16.1	26.8
Single-State Muni. Bond	4.8	10.7
Total Bond & Income	$ 58.7	$130.9
Total Long-Term Funds	137.2	236.3
Money Market	$209.7	$208.1
Limited Maturity Municipal	23.8	39.1
Total Short-Term Funds	233.5	247.2
Total, All Mutual Funds	$370.7	$483.5

*Asset estimates for 1984 are as of the end of the year; 1985 estimates are as of the end of November.

CLOSED-END MANAGEMENT COMPANIES

A closed-end management company is an investment company with a fixed number of shares outstanding. Most closed-end investment companies are listed and traded on exchanges. As a shareholder of such a company, you cannot sell (redeem) your shares back to the fund at net asset value. You can buy or sell the shares at market price, which could be above or below net asset value. Often closed-end funds sell at a (percent) discount from net asset value.

OPEN-END MANAGEMENT COMPANIES

An open-end management company is known as a mutual fund. The number of shares outstanding changes continuously as investors buy additional shares or redeem outstanding shares. There is no limit to the number of shares that the investment company can issue. Shares are bought and sold at net asset value. However, the net proceeds from the sale or the net cost of the purchase depend on whether it is a load or a no-load fund.

NO-LOAD FUNDS

The shares of no-load funds are sold without a sales charge. The purchase price paid by the investor is determined by the net asset value as calculated after the receipt of a purchase order. These funds are especially popular for

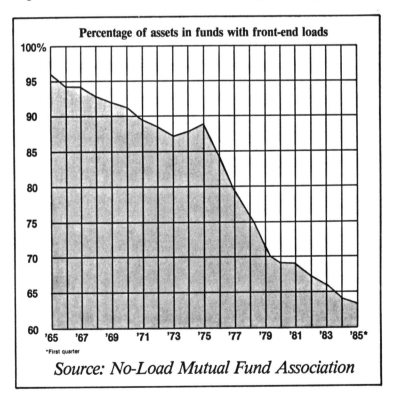

Source: No-Load Mutual Fund Association

trading and switching purposes. With a no-load fund there is no salesperson involved. At present, the majority of investors buy no-load funds.

The total number of no-load mutual funds rose from 150 in 1971 to 600 in 1983. The total no-load mutual funds assets rose from 10 billion in 1971 to 240 billion in 1983. The number of shareowners accounts grew from 1 million in 1971 to 16 million in 1973.

For the past 20 years, funds with upfront sales commissions have been losing ground to no-loads. With the exception of money market funds, assets in funds with initial loads have fallen from 96 percent of the total to 64 percent.

LOAD FUNDS

"Load" is a term used by the mutual fund industry for "sales" charge. The shares of a load fund are purchased at the offering price, which is the net asset value plus a sales charge, through broker-dealers who have sales agreements with the fund distributor. This charge (the load) could vary from fund to fund, up to 8.5 percent of the offering price (approximately 9.3 percent of the net amount invested). The sales charge as a percentage of the offering price usually declines as the amount of purchase increases. If you buy $10,000 of a fund and pay a "load" of 8.5 percent, only $9,150 is invested. The commission of $850 amounts to 9.3 percent of your investment.

FAMILY OF FUNDS

Several mutual fund organizations have a family of funds, each one with a different investment objective. This allows the investor to select a portfolio that fits his or her needs. Usually investors can switch from one fund to another as market condition changes, with minimal or no extra cost. Some of the most common funds include: balanced, fixed income, tax-free income, equity, gold and silver, and money markets.

The purpose of the various funds is to service investors with different investment objectives. The most common objectives are as follows:

1. Balanced funds provide current income from bonds, and some capital gains from common stocks with a reasonable level of risk.
2. Fixed income funds provide a high level of current income through investment in bonds.
3. Tax-free income (municipal bonds) funds provide a high level of tax-exempt current income through investment in municipal bonds.
4. Growth funds offer investors capital appreciation through investment in common stocks.
5. Aggressive growth funds invest in small capitalization growth stocks. (Small capitalization usually refers to companies with less than $100 million in capital. Growth stocks usually refer to the common stocks of companies whose growth rate of sales and earnings is higher than the rate of growth of the economy.)
6. Growth and income funds provide both long-term growth and current income.
7. Option income funds provide total return through option writing strategies.
8. Precious metal funds provide investors a long-term hedge against inflation.
9. Money market funds provide complete liquidity and capital preservation with current income.
10. International funds invest in overseas securities.
11. Qualified corporate dividends funds are specifically designed for corporate cash management needs.
12. Special purpose funds such as social investing are designed to satisfy specific requirements.

You can choose from among many popular fund families: Dreyfus, Fidelity, Neuberger Berman, Stein Roe, Value Line, and Vanguard are just a few examples of funds you can trade. They provide diversification and professional management.

INDEX PORTFOLIO

This refers to a portfolio of securities of a particular market average or a market index. An index fund seeks to mirror the performance of a particular index by matching its portfolio to that of the index. For example, an index portfolio of the S & P 500 includes securities in the S & P 500 index. The rise and fall of the portfolio's value will correspond to changes in the S & P 500 index.

NET ASSET VALUE

The net asset value is calculated by subtracting the liabilities from the value of the fund's portfolio and dividing by the number of shares outstanding. The net asset value is the bid price for mutual funds' shares.

TAX-FREE UNIT TRUSTS

The tax-free unit trust is formed to realize income exempt from federal income taxes and taxable capital gain upon maturity or earlier redemption of the bonds through investment in a fixed, diversified portfolio of long-term bonds issued by or on behalf of states, municipalities, and public authorities. Tax-free unit trusts have been growing in popularity in recent years as many of them are backed by insurance.

Some of the basic features of these trusts are:

- **Diversification.** These trusts offer investors the chance to participate in a portfolio of long-term tax-exempt bonds.
- **Stability.** Standard & Poor's Corporation or Moody's Investors Service, Inc. rate all municipal bonds, when deposited in the portfolio, with an "A" rating or better.

- **Fixed maturity.** When the bonds reach maturity the principal will be paid to the certificateholder.
- **Tax-free income.** All interest income distributed by the trusts are considered free from current federal income taxes, although they may be subject to state and local taxes. Check with your attorney for updated information.
- **Volume discount.** Individuals wishing to purchase more than 100, 500, or 1,000 units receive a discount.
- **Monthly, semiannual, or annual check.** Certificate-holders can receive their interest income checks monthly, semiannually, or annually depending on their investment goals. The monthly checks are helpful for holders who want to spend their interest income, while the other two choices offer a slightly higher yield due to lower administrative charges (since only one or two checks are issued per year).
- **Total reinvestment plan.** Certificateholders who have chosen to receive income seminannually or annually can reinvest the regular interest and principal distribution in fractional units of available series of "Municipal Securities Trust" at a reduced sales charge.

SWITCHING STRATEGIES

Investors may switch from one mutual fund to another or from one portfolio to another within the same series fund. (A series fund is one fund with several portfolios.) Market-timing strategies are often used to determine which portfolio is the best one to own under different market conditions. You could profit by switching between the various types of mutual funds and portfolios such as equity, bonds, income, long-term appreciation, gold, international, option writing, or money market portfolios.

Several mutual funds management organizations have convenient services that let you switch your invest-ment among the funds within the same management group via the telephone. The fund distributor will accept telephone or telegram instructions for the redemption of all or part of any shares in one fund and invest the proceeds in another fund.

When you are concerned about the market, you can switch out of common stock funds and you can "park" your money in a money market fund while waiting for a more attractive environment for equities to develop.

Several brokers have mutual funds services to enable you to buy or sell mutual funds as easily as you trade stocks. You don't have to send the fund a letter or have your signature guaranteed. You can make a phone call with your buy or sell orders. You usually have to pay a small fee to the broker for these services.

ADVANTAGES AND DISADVANTAGES OF MUTUAL FUNDS INVESTING

The following are some of the advantages of investing in mutual funds:

1. You can invest small sums of money. Many funds have a minimum of $500 to $1,000. This could be important, especially when investing in your IRA account.

2. Mutual funds' performance records are readily available so that you can judge if past performances satisfy your investment objectives.

3. Most mutual funds have unique objectives. You can select the one that meets your specific needs.

4. Mutual funds are managed by professionals who have access to research usually not available to the small investor. Each fund shareholder shares the advantages usually available to only wealthier and more sophisticated investors.

5. Diversification is provided, since most funds will invest only a small portion of their assets in one particular security.

6. You can buy mutual funds on margin, and you can borrow money against mutual funds shares in your brokers' account.

7. You can invest in mutual funds for your retirement. You can choose the fund best suited to your personal retirement needs.

The following are some of the disadvantages of investing in mutual funds:

1. The manager of the mutual fund does not know you personally. An investment advisor, on the other hand, will often communicate with you to determine your specific needs.

2. You may get more personal service from a stockbroker or an investment advisor.

3. You have less control in a mutual fund than when you manage your investments personally or with the aid of an investment advisor.

4. Mutual funds incur operating and selling expenses. You, as an investor, are paying your proportionate share of these expenses.

5. You must read the prospectus of each fund carefully and understand the investment restrictions or the costs associated with purchase or redemption of your investment in the fund. In the case of load funds, these costs could be substantial.

SPECIAL SERVICES OFFERED BY MUTUAL FUNDS

Most mutual funds offer the following services:

Automatic reinvestment. This enables you automatically to invest the income received from dividends or capital gains in additional shares of the same fund. This is a common practice among investors. This stimulates dollar averaging if the income is relatively constant.

Exchange privileges. This enables you to transfer the entire or a portion of your investment from one fund to another fund within the same group, or from one portfolio to another portfolio within the same fund.

IRA and Keogh plans. Most funds offer retirement plans for self-employed people and individual retirement accounts to anyone with earned income.

CHAPTER 8

Financial Planning for Your Retirement

THE IMPORTANCE OF PLANNING FOR YOUR RETIREMENT

Planning for your retirement is essential. You should guard against the time when you can no longer work. Savings and investments in stocks and bonds are important considerations for your retirement. Proper planning for retirement may require self-denial of spending, continuous accumulation, and protection of assets from the various risks.

Many people ignore their financial future. According to researchers, six out of ten employees have made no financial plans for retirement. Yet statistics have shown that people are living longer. In 1790, only 2 percent of the nation's population of 3.17 million was over 65. By 1976 that figure had increased to 10.5 percent or 23 million. By the year 2030 one American in five will be over 65.

With all the uncertainties of the coming years, it is important to plan for your retirement. Financial planning should be a family affair. Husbands and wives should participate in making family investment planning decisions.

HOW TO DETERMINE YOUR PERSONAL NET WORTH

How can my personal net worth (assets and liabilities) be determined?

One of the first steps in planning for your retirement is for you to determine where you stand with your assets and liabilities. (Your net worth is equal to your total assets minus your total liabilities.)

Prepare a list of all your assets, including bank accounts, securities at brokerage houses, mutual fund statements, value of life insurance policies, pension, IRA/Keogh, and other retirement plans; real estate holdings, coin or stamp collections, gold/silver investments; etc. Then prepare a list of all your liabilities, including mortgage loans, personal loans, credit card debts, automobile debts, divorce settlement obligations, etc. The determination of your net worth will give you a good idea of how much capital is available for your retirement. This net worth capital has to work for you (produce income for you) during your retirement years. You cannot afford to lose it.

INVESTMENT ADJUSTMENTS

How should I adjust my investments as I approach retirement?

Retired people should take less risk and be more conservative in their investments. They should diversify their portfolios among stocks, bonds, and tax-exempt securities. Their objective should be risk reduction. This includes protection from inflation risk, interest rate risk, etc. Retired people should concentrate on high dividend income and relatively safe investments.

Upon retirement, most investors drop into a lower tax bracket as their income declines. It is wise to switch investments from various tax-free securities to higher yielding taxable securities. This will increase the available after-tax cash flow. For instance, a $10,000 tax-free bond that yields 8.75 percent will generate $875 of after-tax income, regardless of the income tax bracket. A 13 percent taxable bond in a 25 percent tax bracket will generate $975 after-tax income. In this case, a switch from tax-exempt to a taxable investment will generate an additional income of $100.

TAX QUALIFIED RETIREMENT PLAN

For taxable years beginning in 1984, a self-employed individual may make annual tax deductible contributions to a tax-qualified retirement plan of up to 25 percent of self-employed earnings not to exceed $30,000.

INDIVIDUAL RETIREMENT ACCOUNTS (IRAs)

Any individual with earned income, even if presently covered under an employer-sponsored retirement plan, may establish an IRA plan and make annual tax deductible contributions of 100 percent of earned income up to $2,000 (up to $4,000 may be contributed in the case of a married couple who both work and up to $2,250 if contributions are made to separate accounts for the individual and the individual's nonworking spouse). An IRA rollover plan is available to defer taxes on lump sum payments (no maximum amount) received from another retirement plan.

An employer may establish a Simplified Employee Pension IRA for eligible employees and make a minimum annual contribution of 15 percent of earned income (up to $30,000) on behalf of each participant.

What are the advantages of an IRA account?

There are four main advantages: First, your IRA contribution is tax deductible. Your tax savings could be as much as 50 percent, depending on your tax bracket.

Second, the income in your IRA account is not taxed until you begin to withdraw money from your IRA account upon retirement. All earnings are reinvested free of current income tax. You defer paying taxes until the money is withdrawn. The following example illustrates the importance of tax-free accumulation of earnings.

Suppose you contribute $2,000 each January 1, assuming a rate of return of 8 percent or 12 percent for a period of 10, 20, or 30 years with no tax paid in comparison to a 25 percent tax rate.

	Tax-Free		25% Tax	
	8%	12%	8%	12%
After 10 Years	$ 31,828	$ 40,871	$ 21,225	$ 25,570
After 20 Years	$102,477	$175,733	$ 60,051	$ 89,004
After 30 Years	$259,291	$620,730	$131,072	$246,371

This example shows that you can accumulate $620,730 if you did not pay any tax (as would be the case with an IRA) in 30 years. By comparison, you would accumulate only $246,371 if you had to pay a 25 percent tax on your earnings in your savings account.

Third, your IRA contribution could be part of your systematic saving program to help you provide an adequate retirement income. Fourth, by the time you are ready to withdraw without penalty (beginning at age 59½), you will probably be retired or close to considering it. Being retired would place you in a lower tax bracket than when you were working, thus lowering the amount of taxes you will have to pay.

Do I have to contribute a minimum of $2,000 into my IRA account each year?

The maximum amount that you can put into your IRA account each year is $2,000. There is no minimum — anywhere from $1 up to the $2,000 limit is permissible.

What is the deadline for making an IRA contribution?

You must make your total contribution by the date your federal income tax return is due for the year in which you take your IRA deduction.

How much can my spouse contribute to an IRA account?

If you and your spouse are working, and your spouse has compensation or earned income during the taxable year, each of you may contribute 100 percent of your compensation, up to $2,000 each, for a total of $4,000. If you or your spouse does not work, your combined annual IRA contribution could not exceed $2,250. However, the contribution doesn't have to be divided equally between the both of you, although you may not contribute more than $2,000 in any one IRA account.

Who controls the investment decisions in my IRA account?

You control your IRA account. You can decide how you want the money in your IRA account to be invested.

What are the investment alternatives for my IRA?

You may choose from among many available alternative investments. You can open an account with a bank and buy certificates of deposit. You can open an account with a broker and buy securities, common stocks, preferred stocks, or bonds (either zero coupon or high coupon). Since the income from the investment in your IRA is tax-free, you can maximize short-term income without worrying about tax consequences. You could also select a mutual fund with a portfolio that meets your investment objectives. There is no need to invest in tax-advantaged investments in a retirement plan. Oil and gas investments or real estate investments may be more appropriate for your personal portfolio.

CASE IN POINT: Dr. E. needed help managing his Keogh retirement account. His portfolio included restricted stocks (paying no dividends), several diamonds, and few speculative low-quality stocks.

I recommended that he liquidate the holdings in his portfolio and invest the proceeds in high-quality, dividend-paying common stocks and and zero coupon bonds. Unfortunately, losses had to be realized when the old investments were sold. Tax losses cannot be utilized in a retirement plan. (If these investments were purchased in his personal account, at least the losses could be used to offset gains and reduce taxes.)

IRA ROLLOVER

Upon retirement, you can roll over the proceeds from your pension plan to your personal retirement account in a tax-free transaction. If you do not roll over your pension, the proceeds from the liquidation will be taxed at regular tax rates. In effect, this allows you to continue your retirement pension plan.

When can I withdraw money from my IRA account?

You may withdraw money from your IRA account without penalty after age 59½. You may withdraw money before this age, but the amount withdrawn is subject to an IRS penalty tax of 10 percent. Money withdrawn from an IRA account is considered regular taxable income (not capital gain) for federal income tax purposes. Your tax bracket at retirement should probably be lower than it is now. You must start to withdraw money from your IRA at the age of 70½.

What if I die before I have withdrawn all or part of my IRA?

When you open an IRA, you may name a beneficiary to your IRA. You may change the beneficiary at any time by a written notice. The value of your IRA will be paid to your named beneficiary after your death.

RETIREMENT INCOME

Inflation hurts most retired people because they often must depend on fixed retirement income. As prices go up, you as a retired person may have to spend more money to maintain the same standard of living, while at the same time your income may remain unchanged.

In many cases, because of improper financial planning, retired people have to reduce their standard of living. Namely, they can afford to buy fewer goods and services.

INVESTMENTS IN MUTUAL FUNDS

More and more people are choosing mutual funds as an investment vehicle for their retirement. Mutual funds offer a variety of alternatives, including

Money market funds — high current income, preservation of capital, and liquidity

U.S. government reserve funds — high current income, preservation of capital, and liquidity from U.S. government instruments

Income funds — high level of current income from fixed income bonds

Growth funds — capital appreciation from investment in securities with long-term growth potential

Convertible funds — appreciation from investment in securities which are convertible into common stocks

International funds — investment in foreign securities

Gold and silver funds — investment in inflation-hedged securities

IRA investments can be diversified into several mutual funds with a variety of investment objectives. You may shift your retirement assets from one fund to another at any time as changes take place in your investment objective or in market conditions.

INVESTMENT STRATEGIES BY AGE GROUPS

What is the appropriate investment strategy for the various age groups?

Your investment strategy will depend on what stage of your life you are in. You should switch from one strategy to another as you get older.

For children up to age 10: Investments for this age group should be long-term oriented — that is, performance objectives should be realized over a 10- to 15-year period. Zero coupon bonds and long-term growth stocks are appropriate choices.

For ages 10 to 25: Investment for this age group should be most aggressive. Some risk is justified, because current income is usually not the primary consideration. Investment in common stocks is probably the most appropriate choice.

For ages 25 to 45: Investment for this age group should be balanced. Some current income and capital growth are needed. Investment in bonds, convertible bonds, and common stocks with some diversification is recommended. IRAs and other retirement accounts should be initiated.

For ages 45 to 60: Investments for this age group should be conservative. Taxes should be minimized, investments in IRA, Keogh, and other retirement plans should be increased to their maximum, in order to defer taxes. Also, investment in tax-exempt securities should be considered.

For age 60 and over: For this age group, preservation of capital is the most important objective. You do not want to lose your life savings. You are not in a position to earn money that you lose. Investments must be very liquid so that you can sell at any time to provide your needs. You should invest only in high-quality and high-yield bonds, stocks, and money market funds.

A BALANCED PORTFOLIO

In many cases, retired people age 60 and over have a large portion of their assets in tax-free municipal bonds. The main reason for this is that the retired investor needs tax-free income to support living expenses. However, this type of investment is subject to two major risks. One is interest rate risk; the other is inflation risk. Should interest rates go up, the tax-free portfolio will suffer a substantial decline in value. Should inflation reoccur or accelerate, the income generated by this portfolio may not be sufficient to support a desired standard of living level.

CASE IN POINT: Mr. M. is retired at the age of 65. He lives in New York during the summer and in Florida during the winter. His tax-free portfolio is worth about $1 million and generates approximately $90,000 a year in tax-free income. (The average maturity of the bonds in his portfolio is about 25 years.) This income is used to cover living expenses for him and his wife. As long as interest rates decline or remain stable, and as long as inflation is under control, Mr. M. can continue to live very comfortably on his tax-free income. However, should interest rates go up, and should inflation reaccelerate, Mr. M. would not be able to maintain the standard of living to which he is accustomed.

As his investment advisor, I recommended that Mr. M. balance his investment portfolio by selling a portion of his tax-free bonds and invest the proceeds from the sale in asset-oriented investments that would benefit from an increase in the rate of inflation. This includes investing in real estate, real estate securities, oil stocks, and gold and silver stocks. These inflation hedge stocks will go up in value when tax-free bonds go down in value. Therefore, his portfolio is now balanced. I also recommended that maturities of the securities in his portfolio be shortened. A portfolio in which one-third of the bonds mature in seven years, one-third mature in 15 years, and one-third mature in 25 years is much more balanced and involves less risk than a portfolio with average maturity of 25 years.

EDUCATE YOUR HEIRS

Often one member of the family (traditionally the male) has the expertise in investments and finance. Upon that person's death, his or her spouse and children may find themselves with the assets but no knowledge in managing them. It is very important, as part of your overall financial planning for retirement, that you educate your spouse and/or children in financial matters. Have them participate in some of the financial decisions, so they can have some practical experience in financial management.

CHAPTER 9

Tax Planning

CONSULT YOUR ACCOUNTANT OR LAWYER

Tax laws are subject to frequent changes. It is important for you to keep abreast of current tax legislation. You should often consult your accountant or tax lawyer as part of your overall financial planning and to be sure you have the most recent information. Various proposals are presently pending before Congress for changes in the federal and state income tax laws. Such proposals, if enacted into law, could materially affect the manner in which options and related transactions are taxed. It cannot be predicted when or if such legislation will be enacted, or what the ultimate terms or effective date of any legislation might be.

Many investors do not understand fully the tax implications of their investment decisions. Interest received from corporate bonds is fully taxable, but interest received from municipal bonds is free from federal tax and from state taxes if the bonds are issued in the state in which you live.

TREATMENT OF CAPITAL LOSSES

Due to market fluctuations, you may find yourself in a situation where a stock that you wish to own as a long-term investment decreases in value. You can create a tax loss by selling the stock and then buying it back at a later date. You use the tax loss to reduce the taxable income, and you continue to own the stock (after you purchase it).

If I sell a security for tax loss purposes, how long must I wait if I want to buy it back?

At least 31 calendar days, either before or after sale at a loss must elapse in order to avoid a "wash" sale.

What are the tax consequences of a "wash" sale?

A tax loss on sale of a security cannot be realized and must be deferred if you reacquired the security (or a substantially identical security), or entered into a contract or an option to acquire the security during a period beginning 30 days before the sale, and ending 30 days after the sale. The deferral is accomplished by adding to the tax basis of the newly bought security the amount of the loss on the sale.

Can I buy a call option within 30 days of the sale of a stock and still establish a tax loss?

No. Selling the underlying stock at a loss and subsequently buying a call within 30 days on the same stock will disqualify the tax loss.

Treatment of Capital Gains on "Short" Securities Positions

The tax treatment of gains on "short" securities positions is different from the tax treatment of gains on regular long purchases and sale of securities.

Can I realize a long-term gain on a "short" position?

Any capital gain on closing a "short" sale is treated as a short-term gain. Since the short-sale tax rules are designed to prevent investors from converting short-term gains to long-term gains and long-term losses to short-term losses, any gain on closing a short sale is short term — even if an asset (used to close the short sale) is held for more than six months.

Treatment of Capital Losses on "Short" Securities Positions

Where there is a loss on the closing of the "short" sale, the loss is considered as a long-term capital loss if property substantially identical to that sold "short" has been held on the date of the "short" sale for more than one year. This rule applies no matter when the property used to close the short sale was acquired.

TAX TREATMENT OF IRA DISTRIBUTION

If the following takes place in your IRA, your IRA will be disqualified:

1. The lending of money between your IRA and yourself.
2. The sale or exchange of any property between you and your IRA.

The entire balance in your IRA will be treated as if it were distributed to you and will be taxed as ordinary income during the year in which the transaction between your IRA and yourself took place. In addition, you will be subject to a 10 percent penalty tax if you are younger than 59½.

If you pledge part or all of your IRA as collateral against a loan, the portion pledged is treated as distribution and is taxable to you as ordinary income. It is also subject to the 10 percent penalty during the year in which the transaction took place.

A distribution from your IRA to you or to another cannot qualify for capital gain federal tax treatment. A distribution from your IRA is always taxed as ordinary income. However, distribution made to you may qualify for income averaging under current tax laws.

You must also file a Treasury form (5239) with the IRS when a premature distribution takes place.

TAX TREATMENT OF IRA CONTRIBUTION

Regular contributions to your IRA can be claimed as a deduction when you file your tax return forms with the IRS. You can always obtain further information with respect to the tax treatment of IRA contributions and distributions from any district office of the Internal Revenue Service.

TAX SHELTERS

Tax shelters (also known as tax-incentive investments or tax-advantaged investments) are structured in areas where federal tax incentives are applied to give investors a tax advantage when investing in areas such as oil and gas drilling, mining exploration, agriculture, real estate, equipment, and research and development.

Tax shelters usually provide you with current deductions based on investment tax credit, depletion allowances, depreciation, and other deductible expenses.

How do I select a tax shelter?

Real estate, oil and gas, and leasing have become increasingly popular as tax shelter investments. Also, be aware that certain benefits which reduce your regular income tax are "tax preferences" which may subject you to the alternative minimum tax, thereby possibly creating a larger tax liability. Some of these tax preferences are: Accelerated depreciation in excess of straight line, intangible drilling costs, the dividend exclusion, and the 60 percent capital gain deduction. It is important that you take your time and read carefully the "circular offering" describing the risks involved in the tax shelter investment offering. You should always consult your tax, legal, and investment advisors before you invest in a tax shelter. When selecting a tax shelter, you should look not only for tax benefits, but also for the project's future economic profitability.

TAX-FREE SECURITIES

You should always compare the return available from tax-free securities with the return available from taxable securities. Depending on your federal tax bracket, the attractiveness of tax-free income should be evaluated. For example, the following table shows the approximate taxable current returns that taxable securities must earn in various income-tax brackets, to generate an equal return on tax-free securities.

TAXABLE VS. TAX-FREE INCOME
FOR INDIVIDUALS FILING JOINT RETURNS

Return from Taxable Securities for Various Tax Brackets						Equivalent Return from Tax-Free Securities
Federal Tax Bracket						
25%	33%	35%	38%	42%	50%	
11.20	12.54	12.92	13.54	14.48	16.80	8.40
11.60	12.99	13.38	14.03	15.00	17.40	8.70
12.00	13.43	13.84	14.52	15.52	18.00	9.00
12.40	13.88	14.30	15.00	16.03	18.60	9.30
12.80	14.43	14.76	15.48	16.55	19.20	9.60
13.20	14.78	15.23	15.97	17.07	19.80	9.90
13.60	15.22	16.15	16.45	17.59	20.40	10.20

As the above table shows, if you are in the 25 percent tax bracket, an investment in a taxable security yielding a taxable return of 12 percent is equivalent to an investment in a tax-free security with a return of 9 percent.

If you are in a 42 percent tax bracket (in 1985, if you filed a joint return with income of $62,450 to $89,090), a tax-free return of 9.9 percent is equivalent to a taxable return of 17.07 percent.

How will the combination of federal and state taxes affect the tax-free return versus taxable return?

When federal and state income taxes are taken into consideration, the advantages of investing in tax-free securities increase. For example: In the state of New York, a 50.0 percent federal bracket is increased to 59.0 percent (50 percent federal, 14 percent New York State, 4 percent New York City less 7 percent New York State and 2 percent New York City) when federal and state taxes are combined (triple tax free). The maximum for non-residents of New York City is 57 percent (double tax free). A 9.0 percent tax-free return is then equal to a 20.9 percent taxable return (based on 1985 tax rates). In the state of California, a 50.0 percent federal tax bracket is increased to 55.5 percent when federal and state taxes are combined (double tax free). A 9.0 percent tax-free return is then equal to 20.2 percent taxable return (based on 1985 tax rates).

TAX CONSEQUENCES OF AN OPTIONS TRANSACTION

The tax consequences of an options transaction may differ depending upon whether the transaction involves stock options, index options, debt options, or foreign currency options. The tax rules are different for each type, depending on whether the option is exercised or expired or whether the option was sold covered or uncovered. Tax rules are subject to frequent changes. Therefore, you should always consult your accountant or your tax advisor as to the tax consequences of an options transaction.

What are the federal tax aspects of options transactions?

There is a capital gain or loss from sale or exchange of an option or a loss on failure to exercise it only if the property covered by an option is a capital asset in the hands of the taxpayer or would be a capital asset if acquired by him or her. In the case of an option on stock, securities, commodities, or commodity futures, any gain of a non-dealer grantor on the lapse of the options is short-term capital gain. And any gain or loss of a nondealer grantor from a closing transaction is short-term capital gain or loss.

With respect to the writer of a call option, the Internal Revenue Service has ruled that the premium received for selling an option is not included in income at the time of receipt, but is carried in a deferred account until the writer's obligation expires through the passage of time, until the writer sells the underlying stock pursuant to the exercise of a call, or until the writer engages in a closing transaction.

What is the tax treatment when I sell an option?

If your obligation as a writer (seller) of an option expires through the passage of time or through a closing transaction, the premium constitutes short-term capital gain upon such expiration. A loss on expiration of a call or a put is a short-term capital loss.

If the writer of an option engages in a closing transaction by payment of an amount equivalent to the value of the option at the time of such payment, the difference between the amount so paid and the premium received constitutes short-term capital gain or loss.

If the call option is exercised, the premium received is treated as part of the proceeds of the sale of the underlying stock. Gain or loss on such sale is capital gain or loss and is short-term or long-term, depending on the holding period of the stock involved.

If a call is written at a time when the underlying stock (or a call thereon) has been held by the taxpayer for six months or less, or if the underlying stock is acquired after a call is written and before exercise or expiration of the call so written, the writing of the call does not affect the holding period of the underlying stock.

What is the tax treatment when I buy an option?

When you own (are long) a call or a put for more than six months, a closing transaction or an expiration of the option is treated as long-term capital gain or loss. When the call is exercised, the cost of the call is added to the cost of the purchased stock. When the put is exercised, the cost of the put is subtracted from the amount realized from the sale of the stock.

What are the holding period requirements for capital assets?

The holder of a capital asset is entitled to long-term capital gain or loss treatment on disposition of such asset only if, among other requirements, he satisfies the applicable long-term holding period requirements of the Internal Revenue Code; otherwise, the gain or loss on disposition of a capital asset is short-term capital gain or loss. With respect to a disposition of a capital asset (including underlying stock) in a taxable year beginning in 1978 or thereafter, a taxpayer is entitled to long-term capital gain or loss treatment if the capital asset has been held for more than one year (for assets acquired prior to June 22, 1984) as of the disposition. If the asset was acquired after June 22, 1984, it qualifies for long-term treatment if held for more than six months. The holding period for stock purchased or stock options begins on the day after the date of purchase and includes the date of the sale.

Will the holding period of the underlying stock be affected by the purchase of a put?

Yes. The purchase of a put will terminate (for tax purposes) the holding period of the stock. For example: you held the stock for three months. You bought a put and continue to own the stock. Your holding period will be short-term (although you continue to own the stock) because you bought the put.

A January 40 put was sold on December 10, 1984 at 5. The put expired (was not exercised). What is the tax treatment of this transaction?

The gain of $500 is short-term for the tax year 1985.

QUALIFIED CORPORATE DIVIDEND

If you own or control a corporation, or if you are a financial officer of a corporation, you should be aware of the tax advantages of investing your corporate cash reserve in a dividend-paying preferred stock. Corporations can retain tax-free 93.1 percent of the qualified dividends received from an investment in another corporation, and pay a federal tax of only 6.9 percent. (This is at a corporate tax rate of 46 percent on 15 percent taxable dividends after utilizing the 85 percent dividends-received deduction.)

Shareholders on record date are entitled to receive dividends. To qualify for the intercorporate 85 percent dividend deduction, the stock must be held for at least 46 calendar days.

DIVIDENDS, CAPITAL GAINS DISTRIBUTIONS, AND TAX STATUS OF MUTUAL FUNDS

Payments to you as a shareholder, which are classified by a mutual fund as long-term capital gains distribution, will be taxed to you as long-term capital gain regardless of how long you have held the shares of the fund. However, if you hold shares in a fund for six months or less, any loss on the sale of the shares will be treated as long-term capital loss to the extent of the long-term capital gains distribution received by you. Most funds will mail you information concerning the federal income tax status of dividends and distributions at least once a year.

The policy of most funds is to distribute to its shareholders at least 90 percent of its investment company taxable income, if any, 90 percent of its excess of interest excludable from gross income under Section 103 of the Internal Revenue Code of 1954, as amended (the "Code") over its deductions disallowed under Code Sections 265 and 171(a)(2), if any, and any net realized capital gains for each year. This is done to meet the distribution requirements of Part I of Subchapter M of the Code.

Most mutual funds comply with the diversification requirements of assets and sources of income so that they don't pay any taxes on net investment income and net realized capital gains paid to their shareholders.

Dividends and capital gains distribution paid by the funds to you as a shareholder are subject to taxation as of the date of payment, whether received by you in cash or in shares of the funds, and whether representing an ordinary distribution or one classified as from long-term capital gains. Dividends paid by mutual funds from their taxable income, including net short-term capital gains, are taxable to you as a shareholder at ordinary income tax rates based on your tax bracket. The portion paid to you in cash, which is attributable to dividends from domestic corporations, is at present eligible for $100 dividend exclusion ($200 for joint return). This exclusion is subject to change, so be sure to consult your tax advisor for the most up-to-date information. If a corporation is a shareholder of the fund, it is entitled to the 85 percent dividends received deduction available to corporate shareholders. This is subject to possible change under current proposed legislation.

Premiums from expired call options written by mutual funds and net gain or loss from closing purchase transactions are treated as short-term capital gain or loss for federal income tax purposes. However, a short-term loss is realized when the fund closes certain in-the-money covered call transactions involving equity securities which will be converted to a long-term capital loss if a sale of the underlying security on the date of such transaction will have given rise to a long-term capital gain or loss. If a written call option is exercised, the premium is added to the proceeds of the sale and the underlying security, and the gain or loss from such sale will be short-term or long-term, depending on the period such security was held. If a put option which the fund has written is exercised, the amount of the premium originally received will reduce the cost of the security, which the mutual fund purchases upon exercise of the option.

If an option on an equity security which the mutual fund has purchased expires on the stipulated expiration date, the fund will realize a short-term capital loss for federal income-tax purposes in the amount of the cost of the option. If the fund enters a closing sale transaction with respect to such an option, it realizes a capital gain or loss, depending on whether the sale proceeds from the closing sale transaction are greater or less than the cost of the option. The gain or loss will be short-term or long-term, depending on the fund's holding period in the option. If the fund exercises a put option on an equity security, it will realize a gain or loss (long-term or short-term, depending on the period for which the fund has held the underlying security prior to the time it purchased the put) from the sale of the underlying security and the proceeds from such sale will be decreased by the premium originally paid. However, since the purchase of a put option is treated as a short-sale for federal income tax purposes, the holding period of a hedged underlying security will be terminated by such purchase and will start again only when the fund enters a closing sale transaction with respect to such option or it expires. If a fund exercises a call option on an equity security, the premium paid for the option will be added to the cost of the security purchased.

If a fund is invested in any foreign currency contract, the principles of marking-to-market apply to the contract, in that the contract is treated as having been sold for its fair market value on the last business day of the fund's taxable year, giving rise to a capital gain or loss. Sixty percent of any net gain or loss recognized on the deemed sale, as well as 60 percent of the gain or loss with respect to the foreign currency contracts on any termination (including expiration) of the contract will be treated as long-term capital gain or loss, and the remaining 40 percent will be treated as short-term capital gain or loss.

Realized short-term capital gains, including net premiums from expired options, net gains from closing purchase transactions, and net short-term gains from securities sold upon the exercise of options or otherwise, less any net realized long-term capital losses, will be distributed by most funds quarterly with the same record and payment dates as the fund's income dividends. You should consult your tax advisor concerning the application of state and local taxes.

TAX PLANNING: SOME IMPORTANT DEADLINE DATES

A missed tax deadline could cause you unnecessary taxable income in a given year. Although the following list of deadlines is subject to change, it can help you plan for the future:

December 23
- Last day for sale of stock at a gain (regular way)
- Last day for buy-in to close short position in stock at a gain or loss (regular way)

December 30
- Last day to buy-in to close short position in listed option at a gain or loss
- Last day for sale of listed options at a gain

December 31
- Start a new Keogh Plan
- Last day for sale of stock and listed options at a loss

April 15   • Contribute to an existing Keogh Plan.
                    However, this contribution may be
                    made by the actual filing date of the
                    return if an extension in time is ob-
                    tained.
                  • Start and/or contribute to the past year's
                    IRA

NOTE: Selling stock the "regular way" refers to the
industry term for a normally accepted settlement date.
Settlement is due on the fifth business day following the
stock trade date.

CHAPTER 10

Future Outlook

CONCENTRATION OF INVESTMENT DECISION-MAKERS

The securities market is now dominated by large institutions (e.g., banks, mutual funds, insurance companies). As a result, large sums of money are now controlled by few managers. In 1965, big block trades (10,000 shares or more) accounted for 0.31 percent of the New York Stock Exchange volume. By 1976, that percentage had risen to 18.7 percent. In 1985, that percentage had exceeded half of the trading on the New York Stock Exchange. (See illustration on page 158.)

The average number of shares per trade on the New York Stock Exchange in 1962 was 204. In 1984, the average trade was 1,781 shares, indicating the relative decline in public trading and a concentrated increase in institutional trading. Should this trend continue, the market will be subject to increased short-term price volatility of securities. This will result in an added risk to the small investor.

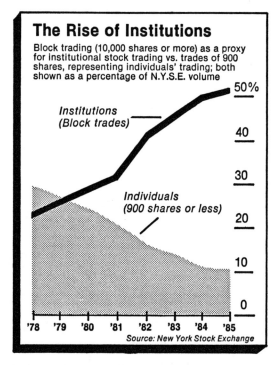

The Rise of Institutions

Block trading (10,000 shares or more) as a proxy for institutional stock trading vs. trades of 900 shares, representing individuals' trading; both shown as a percentage of N.Y.S.E. volume

Institutions (Block trades)

Individuals (900 shares or less)

50%
40
30
20
10
0

'78 '79 '80 '81 '82 '83 '84 '85

Source: New York Stock Exchange

    Professional portfolio managers are human and subject to the same "herd instinct" as the general public. Should these few managers decide, at the same time, to sell a particular stock or a group of stocks, it could create an imbalance of sell orders to be followed by a sharp decline in prices. Vice versa, should these few decision makers buy at the same time a particular stock or a group of stocks, it would create an imbalance of buy orders to be followed by a sharp increase in prices. This trend of concentration could have a negative effect on the concept of a free trading-market behavior.

Put and Call Options

    The recent popularity of put-and-call options trading has affected the nature of investment, as more and more investment managers are using options as a hedging tool. This is especially true in the last few days before the expiration date of options.

Index Futures

Buying and selling index futures by index funds to improve their performance could create unusual price volatility before the expiration date of index futures. The unwinding programs associated with hedging securities with index futures creates a sharp price movement during the last day when traders rush to close open positions.

Too Much Information

Due to technological advances in communication, people today have instant access to data-base information through home and office computers, television, satellites, and other modern equipment. Having too much information can sometimes be as damaging as having too little. It can confuse the decision-maker and detract from the relevant issues. As you save and accumulate financial assets, and weigh the investment risks involved, remember that there is no easy way to financial success.

Social Changes That Can Affect Investment

Average American	1935	1985
Average Age:	27	31
Life Expectancy:	61	75
Annual Earnings:	$1,137	$12,788
Hourly Wages:	$0.45	$8.83
Life Insurance Coverage:	$2,160	$17,380
Old-Age Assistance (monthly)	$15.57	$449
Fellow Americans	127,521,000 (48 states)	238,631,000 (50 states)
Marriages During Year:	1,098,000	2,487,000
Divorces During Year:	218,000 (20% of marriages)	1,550,000 (62% of marriages)
College Enrollments During Year:	1,055,360	12,247,000

Food Consumption*:

Meat:	117	176
Fresh Fruit:	133	95
Fresh Vegetables:	111	78
Ice Cream:	8	18
Number of Daily Newspapers:	1,950	1,701
Number of Golf Courses in U.S.:	332	13,084
Percentage of Population in Prison:	0.1%	6.7%

---

*Per capita; in pounds; annually.

Source of Table: "A Half-Century of Progress," *Dollar$ense*, Fall 1985.

These social changes may or may not continue as indicated in the table. However, investment opportunities will always exist. Companies with new technologies will continue to emerge and older established companies will gradually disappear.

GLOBAL INVESTING

Investors around the world will be able to trade, within the next few years, any major stock at any hour. Around the clock trading of major corporations will be feasible as the foreign exchanges, such as the London Stock Exchange, will be sharing information and price quotes with the American National Association of Securities Dealers.

The London trading hours begin at 4:30 a.m. New York time. Although the American exchanges are closed then, investors will have access to prices at which London market-makers will buy and sell stocks such as IBM, GE, or GM.

Investors will look for investment opportunities worldwide. Americans will invest in Japanese or European companies to diversify their holdings and to hedge against a decline in the dollar. Similarly, foreign investors will invest in U.S. corporations because they consider the U.S. to be a safe environment.

The following table illustrates price trends on the world's major stock markets, as calculated by Capital International S.A., Geneva. To make them directly comparable, each index is based on the close of 1969 equaling 100.

	1969	1984	1985	% Change 1984-1985
U.S.	100	190	191	+ 20.2
Britain	100	428	427	+ 20.9
Canada	100	305	307	+ 15.6
Japan	100	573	573	+ 8.4
France	100	254	252	+ 30.8
Germany	100	224	224	+ 64.5
Hong Kong	100	1168	1151	+ 43.8
Switzerland	100	174	175	+ 45.1
Australia	100	186	184	+ 40.6
World Index	100	245	244	+ 30.7

As the table shows, an investment in the German market in 1985 would have yielded the best percentage gain with 64.5 percent.

OVER-THE-COUNTER THIRD MARKET TRADING

With the development of computer communications systems, you will see an increase in trading over the counter including trading of listed stocks in the "third market." The number of trading hours will expand to include 24 hours to accommodate the need of international investors' needs.

A MULTITUDE OF INVESTMENT ALTERNATIVES

Numerous investment alternatives are available. During periods of a declining rate of inflation or deflation, sustained economic growth and a favorable tax environment, financial assets (bonds, treasury securities, and

stocks) outperform tangible assets (gold, silver, farm land,
oil, diamonds, and housing). During periods of rapid
inflation and high rate of taxes, tangible assets outperform
financial assets.

For example, the compounded annual rate of return
over the past 15 years from bonds was about +7 percent.
Yet, from June 1, 1984 to June 1, 1985, the annual return
from bonds was +42 percent. In the case of silver, the
annual rate of return over the past 15 years was about +7
percent. Yet from June 1, 1984 to June 1, 1985 the price of
silver declined by about 35 percent. In the case of Treasury
bills, the average annual return over the past 15 years was
the same from June 1, 1984 to June 1, 1985. The following
table shows the rate of return of different investment
alternatives over a one-year period and a 15-year period.

Investment Alternative	Annual Return	
	1969-1984 15 Years (%)	6/1/84 to 6/1/85 (%)
oil	+20	- 5
U.S. coins	+17	+10
gold	+15	-22
stamps	+13	-10
diamonds	+ 8	+ 0
silver	+ 7	-35
bonds	+ 7	+42
stocks	+ 7	+30
Treasury bills	+ 7	+ 7
housing	+ 6	+ 3
farm land	+ 3	-12
foreign exchange	+ 3	-12

As the stock market changes to accommodate progress, the need for financial specialists increases. It's not
unlike the family doctor. At the turn of the century, the
average American went to his general practitioner for all
sorts of ailments ranging from headaches to back problems

to foot disorders. As medicine progressed, more and more physicians began to specialize in specific areas. Now it's not uncommon for the average American to see several different physicians: an optometrist, an internist, a podiatrist. Different professionals for different needs.

The same may apply to the field of financial planning and investments in the future. You may need to seek the advice of various investments specialists to determine which alternative is best for you at any given period of time. For example, there may be financial specialists in precious metals, tax-exempt securities, mutual funds investments, investment banking, technology, and so on.

There are some aspects of human behavior that will never change. Basic emotions such as fear, greed, over-optimism or overpessimism, and the desire to get rich quick will continue to be important factors to consider in the securities market.

One thing we can say with great certainty — the securities market will continue to fluctuate.

THE 1929 STOCK MARKET CRASH: COULD IT HAPPEN AGAIN?

Yes. Despite the checks and balances that were introduced after the Great Depression, such as unemployment insurance, intervention by the Federal Reserve, monetary policies, government spending and fiscal policies, we will probably see a repeat of the 1929 stock market crash sometime during the next decade.

For example, let's look at what happened to the stock of two major U.S. companies in the 1920s. The common stock of American Telephone and Telegraph (AT&T) rose from about $140 in 1926 to $310 in 1929. It then dropped to about $70 in 1932 — a drop of 240 points or 77.4 percent. The common stock of Sears Roebuck rose from $11 in 1926 to $49 in 1928. It then dropped to about $2.50 in 1932 — a drop of 46.5 points or 94.8 percent. (See next page.)

AMERICAN TELEPHONE AND TELEGRAPH
PRICE PER SHARE 1926-1946

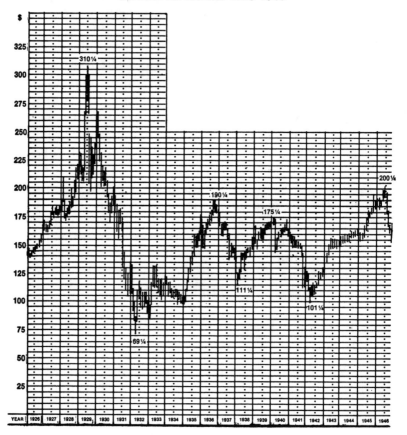

The U.S. economy and the securities market face several major problems:

1. Federal budget deficits
2. Debt of foreign countries
3. Low personal savings rate
4. Low productivity
5. Balance of trade deficits
6. High level of real interest rates

**SEARS ROEBUCK
PRICE PER SHARE 1926-1946**

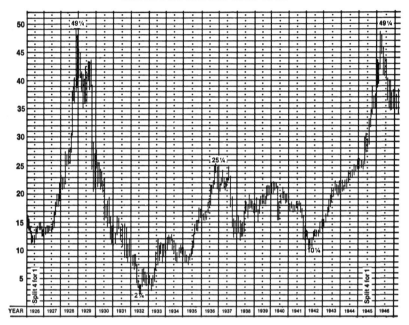

What the U.S. economy needs is a sharp increase in productivity, a much higher level of personal saving. In 1985, the U.S. saving rate declined to 3 percent, while the Japanese saving rate was near 15 percent.

As the chart (page 166) shows, the U.S. personal saving rate has declined from the 9-10 percent level in 1974-1975 to the 3 percent level in 1985

Other factors to consider are the increase of investments in industrial equipment (corporate savings); reduction in personal, corporate, and government debt; and a reduction in the level of consumption. In addition, large cuts in federal spending are necessary to cut the budget deficit.

It is unlikely that the above will take place, because people for the most part are not willing to sacrifice their standard of living. Therefore, I expect a major financial crisis to occur during the next decade. You should prepare yourself for this eventuality.

PERSONAL SAVINGS RATE — 1970 TO 1985

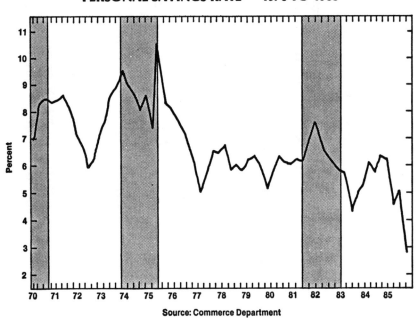

Source: Commerce Department

Glossary

ACCRUED INTEREST. Interest due from the last payment to the present day. When you buy a bond, you must pay the seller the accrued interest, and when you sell, the buyer pays you the accrued interest.

ACCUMULATION. A process describing investor absorption of a supply of securities over a period of time. It usually occurs after a decline in the price of a security. Although there is often little change in price during accumulation periods, a favorable uptrend develops once the accumulation is over. One measure of accumulation is On-Balance Cumulative Volume.

AGAINST THE BOX. The "short sale" of a security which the investor already owns. The stock which is owned is often held for long-term appreciation and can also be used to cover the short sale. An investor may "sell short" against the box when the long-term outlook for the stock is bullish but the near-term outlook is bearish, or when capital gain is to be protected.

AGGREGATE EXERCISE PRICE. The striking price of an option contract multiplied by the number of units of the underlying stock.

ALERT. A signal or warning to alert the investor that unusual (statistically nonrandom) behavior is occurring in the stock. This warning signal may affect the investor's decision to buy, hold, or sell.

ALERT (Price). Unusual (nonrandom) price behavior that alerts the investor to changes in trend. For example, a stock might break through a 200-day moving average on the downside or on the upside. The investor should be alerted that a new price trend has developed. The stock might also break through support or resistance levels indicating that a new trend is in progress.

ALERT (Volume). Unusual (nonrandom) volume behavior that alerts the investor to changes in supply or demand. This becomes apparent when high volume occurs on either the downside or the upside. Unusual behavior might refer to a sudden fivefold increase in a daily volume as compared with the average daily volume for the last six months.

ARBITRAGE. The simultaneous purchase of securities in one market and sale in another to take advantage of a price differential. In an arbitrage the investor attempts to buy a relatively underpriced security and sell short a relatively overpriced security. On occasion, the buy side can be a stock and the sell side a convertible bond, because the stock is selling for less than the value that could be obtained by converting the bond. Profits are achieved when the relative positions move back to a normal relationship.

ASKED. The price at which securities are offered by sellers to potential buyers.

BACKING AND FILLING. The action of the market when there is no discernible action, either up or down. It represents a trendless or a sideway market.

BALANCE SHEET. Financial statement showing the company's assets, liabilities, and net worth (shareholders' equity) as determined on one specific day; for example, "The Balance Sheet for ABC Company, as of December 31, 19X7." It is a picture of the company's financial condition at one specific time of the year.

BAR CHART. A price chart which represents high-low-close data as bars on the vertical axis and time intervals on the horizontal axis. Volume is indicated as vertical bars at the bottom of the chart under the applicable price data.

BASIS POINTS. One hundred basis points represent 1 percent in interest yield. Often used by professionals to measure small changes in bond yield.

BEAR-BULL CYCLE. A stock market cycle that combines both a bear market period and a bull market period.

BEAR MARKET. When the general trend of securities prices is down over a long period of time (six months to one year).

BEAR SPREAD. The investor will buy the higher exercise price and sell the lower exercise price. The spreader hopes that the price of the underlying stock will decline. The investor anticipates that the spread will narrow.

BEARISH TIME SPREAD. When the investor buys the more distant option and sells the nearby option, with the same exercise prices. This is undertaken when the price of the underlying stock is above the exercise price but is expected to decline.

BETA (β). A measure of stock volatility in relation to market volatility; i.e., the relationship between the price fluctuation of a specific stock and the overall fluctuation in the New York Stock Exchange's composite average. A beta below 1 indicates that the stock is more stable than the market; a beta above 1 indicates that the stock is more volatile than the market. For example, a beta of 1.2 means that when the market goes up 5% the stock is expected to go up 6%: if the stock market is down 1% the stock is expected to be down 1.2%.

BID. The price buyers offer to pay potential sellers for securities.

BLOCK. The New York Stock Exchange defines transactions of 10,000 shares or more as blocks.

BLOCK LIQUIDITY. Refers to the concession on downtick blocks. Also used as a guide to market liquidity.

BLOCKS (Opening). The first transaction of the day in a particular stock. It often represents an accumulation of individual buy and sell orders but appears on the tape as a single transaction.

BLUE-CHIP STOCKS. Represent well-known established companies that are leaders in their respective industries. They are usually considered as relatively stable, safe investments.

BONDS. Represent debt obligations or liabilities with specific maturity dates and stated rate of interest. Bonds are a promise to pay. The bond indenture is a legal agreement between the corporation (borrower) and the bondholders (creditors).

BREADTH (Market). Number of advancing stocks minus the number of declining stocks. When advances exceed declines, breadth is positive. When declines exceed advances, breadth is negative. Market breadth statistics for the week include Issues Traded, Advances, Declines, New Highs, and New Lows.

BREAKOUT (Price). When the price of a specific stock breaks away from a trading range; i.e., when it breaks a resistance level on the upside or support level on the downside. An all-time high breakout means that the stock is trading at a new high (never traded before at this level). Sometimes a breakout also refers to a stock crossing its moving average.

BREAKOUT (Volume). Refers to a new high in a series of on-balance volume figures. Such volume breakouts often precede price breakouts; an upside breakout is bullish while a downside breakout is considered bearish.

BULL MARKET. When the general trend of securities prices is up over an extended period of time (six months to one year).

BULL SPREAD. The investor will buy the lower exercise price and sell the higher exercise price. The spreader hopes that the price of the underlying stock will rise. The investor anticipates that the spread will widen.

BULLISH TIME SPREAD. When the investor buys the more distant option and sells the nearby option with the same exercise prices. It is used by investors when the stock is expected to rise.

BUY BACK. The purchase transaction by which you, as the writer of an option, liquidate your position as a writer. Thus, you free yourself from the obligation.

BUY-IN. A situation which occurs when a short seller is forced to cover if no stock can be borrowed to maintain a short position, or when the writer of a naked call has to buy the shares to deliver when the call is exercised.

CALENDAR SPREAD. Also known as horizontal spread or time spread. Simultaneous purchase and sale of option contracts in the same underlying stock, with the same exercise price, but with different expiration dates.

CALL OPTION. An option to buy.

CALL LOANS. Bank loans to brokers. These loans are backed by securities and are to be paid on demand.

CAPITAL GAIN/LOSS. The proceeds from the sale of securities minus the cost of the purchase. If the sale is more than the cost of the purchase, it is a capital gain; if the sale is less than the cost, it is a capital loss.

CATS (Certificate of Accrual on Treasury Securities). Certificates that represent ownership in serially maturing interest payments and principal payments on United States Treasury Notes or Bonds. The Coupon Obligations and Principal Obligations are Direct Obligations of the United States of America. Owners of Coupon CATS and Principal CATS receive a single payment at maturity. CATS are offered in registered form in face amounts of $1,000 and integral multiples of $1,000.

CBOE. Chicago Board of Options Exchange.

CERTIFICATES OF DEPOSIT. Time deposits with guaranteed interest rates, usually with terms of three months to five years.

CHART. There are two main types of charts: a bar chart, and a point and figure chart. See *Bar Chart* and *Point and Figure* for more information.

CHICAGO BOARD OF OPTIONS EXCHANGE (CBOE). The Chicago Board of Options Exchange was founded in 1973 for the purpose of trading call options. It offers investors a continuous auction market where options may be bought and sold. Even with trading limited to options on only a selected list of underlying stocks, the CBOE is very active and has generated a great deal of interest among investors.

CLASS OF OPTIONS. A group of options covering the same underlying security.

CLEARING MEMBER. Refers to a member of an exchange who is a member of the Options Clearing Corporation.

CLIMAX. The end of a trend which is indicated by high price volatility and a relatively high level of volume activity.

CLOSING PURCHASE TRANSACTION (Option). A transaction performed by the writer of an option in order to terminate an option obligation. The option purchased is of the same series as the option previously written. In effect, the writer's preexisting position is canceled.

CLOSING SALE TRANSACTION (Option). A transaction performed by the holder of an outstanding option in order to liquidate a position. The option sold is of the same series as the option previously purchased. In effect, the holder's preexisting position is liquidated.

COLLATERAL. Property (related or unrelated) pledged to secure debt obligations or obligations entered into under an option contract.

COMBINATION OPTION. An option strategy that combines two or more basic option strategies. For example, an investor purchases a 50 call option and also purchases a 70 put option. Because the two option exercise prices (call and put) are different, it is a combination.

COMMERCIAL PAPER. Unsecured, noninterest bearing short-term notes of corporations. They are issued and traded at a discount from face value.

CONCESSION. The decision to permit a price differential between trades when a block or blocks of stock are involved.

CONSOLIDATION. A reaction, a short-term correction or a resting stage within a trend, with the expectation that the trend will resume in the same direction. A consolidation usually lasts for only a short period of time.

CONVERSION. The change of a call to a put or a put to a call.

CONVERTIBLE SECURITIES. There are two kinds of convertible securities: convertible bonds and convertible preferred stocks. As the owner of either a convertible bond or a preferred stock, you have the privilege to convert it to another security (usually common stock) of the issuing company within a given period of time and at a specific rate of exchange.

COVERED CALL. A call for which you own the stock on which you sell the call option.

COVERING (Stock). Purchase of a stock in the open market to replace shares sold short.

CUMULATIVE PREFERRED STOCK. As the owner of a preferred stock, you are assured that before any dividend is paid to the common stock shareholder, you will be paid a preferred stock dividend. Cumulative preferred means that if a corporation skips and does not pay its current preferred dividend, it will be paid in the future (all arrears dividends not paid) before any common shareholder gets any dividends.

DAY ORDER. An order to buy and sell securities that expires at the end of the day. If the order is not executed during the day, it is automatically canceled. In a GTC (good till canceled) order, the order is still open even if not executed that same day. The order will remain open until canceled.

DELIVERY VERSUS PAYMENT. Securities that are purchased through a broker are delivered to a custodian bank against payment. The securities are kept with the bank for the investor's account rather than with the broker. However, this delivery involves additional cost. Therefore, many small investors often prefer to keep their securities with their brokers.

DIFFUSION INDEX. Refers to the percentage of stocks above their 10-week moving average.

DISTRIBUTION. A distribution pattern describes the process of investor supply overcoming demand during a specific period of time. Distribution often is accompanied by high volatility in price movement followed later by a downtrend.

DIVERGENCE. A market index move which deviates from the norm or from another market index and which may be followed by a market adjustment. Historically, there are usually a few months of divergence when several averages move to new highs, while other averages decline before a top forms.

DIVIDENDS. Can be either cash or stock dividends. Cash dividends are paid by corporations to shareholders. Dividends are paid after they are declared by a company's board of directors; corporations are not obligated to pay dividends, as in the case of interest on bonds. Stock dividends are payments of additional shares to shareholders.

DOW JONES INDUSTRIAL AVERAGE. The 30 blue-chip industrial stocks used in the Dow Jones Industrial Average are: Allied Corp., Alcoa, Amer. Can, Amer. Express, AT&T (new), Bethlehem Steel, Chevron, Dupont, Eastman Kodak, Exxon, General Electric, General Motors, Goodyear, INCO, IBM, Int'l.

Harvester, Int'l. Paper, McDonald's, Merck, Minnesota Min. & Mfg., Owens-Illinois, Philip Morris, Procter & Gamble, Sears Roebuck, Texaco, Union Carbide, U.S. Steel, United Tech, Westinghouse, Woolworth.

DOW JONES TRANSPORTATION AVERAGE. The 20 stocks used in the Dow Jones Transportation Average are: AMR Corp, Burlington Northern, Canadian Pacific, Carolina Freight, Consolidated Freight, CSX Corp., Delta Air, Eastern Airline, Federal Express, Norfolk Southern, Northwest Air, Overnight Transportation, Pan-Am, Rio Grande Ind., Santa-Fe Southern Pacific, Transway Int'l., Trans World, UAL, Union Pacific, U.S. Air.

DOW JONES UTILITIES AVERAGE. The 15 stocks used in the Dow Jones Utilities Average are: Amer. Elec. Power, Cleveland Electric, Columbia Gas, Commonwealth Edison, Consolidated Edison, Consolidated Natural Gas, Detroit Edison, Houston Industries, Niagara Mohawk Power, Pacific Gas & Elec., Panhandle Eastern, Peoples Energy, Philadelphia Electric, Public Service Elec. & Gas, Southern Calif. Edison.

The stocks included in the above averages may change from time to time.

DOWNTICK. The transaction that takes place at a price lower than that of the previous transaction.

DOWNTICK (Zero). The transaction which takes place at the same price as the previous transaction, but lower than the last different price.

DOWNTREND. A term that refers to downward movement of a "time series" of data over a specific period of time.

ERISA. Employee Retirement Income Security Act, passed in 1974.

EXCHANGE TRADED OPTION. A call option traded on an exchange. An exercise notice must be properly filed with the Option Clearing Corporation prior to the fixed expiration date of the option.

EX-DIVIDEND DATE. The investor who buys a stock on or after the ex-dividend date is not entitled to the dividends. The investor who purchases a stock before the ex-dividend date is entitled to receive the dividend. Newspaper tabulation of stock prices are adjusted to take into account ex-dividend in the following manner. If the stock trades ex-dividend $.25, and closes ⅝ lower than the previous day, the papers will report the stock down ⅜, (-⅝ plus $.25) and not down ⅝. When stocks trade ex-dividend, especially when the dividend is a large one, there may be an opening price gap. This type of a gap is of no significance if it is not larger than the amount of the dividend.

EXERCISE PRICE. The price at which the holder of a call option or a put option can buy or sell the underlying stock. The price is set at the time the option contract originates. It is subject to adjustment under certain circumstances.

EXPIRATION DATE. The last day on which the owner of an option can exercise it and buy (in the case of a call) or sell (in the case of a put) 100 shares of the underlying stock. The option becomes worthless after the expiration date. CBOE options expire quarterly on either the January, April, July, October cycle or the February, May, August, November cycle. All options expire on the Saturday following the third Friday of the expiration month. Options are traded in the nearest three of the four expiration months in its cycle.

EXPONENTIAL SMOOTHING CALCULATIONS. A forecasting technique based on a weighted moving average calculation, which is updated periodically (daily, weekly, or monthly). The average is a weighted sum of all past data with a certain specific weight being placed on the most recent information. The estimate of the new average is obtained by use of the following formula: N.A. = O.A. + (N.D. - O.A.) × Alpha. The new average (N.A.) is equal to the old average (O.A.) plus the difference between the new data (N.D.)

and the old average (O.A.) multiplied by a fraction (called Alpha). The advantage of the exponential smoothing technique is that it does not require keeping a detailed historical record in an active computer file, thereby cutting down on data processing time.

EXTENDED. A stock is extended when it is near or beyond a trend channel line or when the ratio of its price to its 200-day moving average is above normal. When this takes place the probability for a price correction is high.

FACE VALUE. The value written on the face of the security. In bonds, it is the amount the holder receives when the bond matures. Also called par value.

FUNDAMENTAL ANALYSIS. Fundamental analysis looks at the underlying values of a company itself. It examines earnings per share, book value, price/earning ratio, dividends and yields, statements of assets and liabilities and profit and loss, research and development effectiveness, the introduction of new products where applicable, plant capacity where applicable, and competition. The above may apply to one company, an industry or the market as a whole. In addition, historical trends for the same factors are analyzed and future projections are made. Fundamentals are especially important in evaluating the potential downside risk of the stock or of the market as a whole. It is also important for long-term buy and hold strategies. Fundamental Analysis is less important in making short-term option trading decisions.

FUTURES MARKET (INTEREST RATE FUTURES). The Chicago Board of Trade introduced interest rate futures in 1975. Interest rate futures are used on a regular basis by securities dealers, commercial banks, thrifts, insurance companies, pension funds, mortgage bankers, corporations, and individual investors. Each finds in interest rate futures an effective and efficient mechanism to hedge risk in the highly volatile financial markets. Interest rate futures can be used to protect or "hedge" a current or anticipated investment in fixed income securities. This is accomplished by taking a futures position opposite the cash position. (An inverse relationship exists between interest rates and the price or value of the debt instrument. As rates rise, prices decline; as rates fall, prices advance.)

The following are all actively trading in the futures market: grains such as wheat, corn, oats, soybeans; metals such as copper, gold, and silver; livestock such as cattle, pork bellies, and hogs; foods such as coffee, orange juice, and sugar; industrials such as lumber, cotton, and heating oil; and stock indexes such as value line, S&P 500, NYSE composite, and the major market index.

GAP. A gap occurs when the price range for a given day does not overlap the price range for the previous day. It represents a discontinuity in the price movement and defines the price range where no shares are traded. Usually the daily range (high-low) of trading overlaps part of the previous daily range of trading.

GAP (Breakout). A gap that signals the start of a price move of the security.

GAP (Down). Occurs when today's highest price minus yesterday's lowest price exceeds zero.

GAP (Exhaustion). A gap that signals the end of a move.

GAP (Runaway). A gap that marks the continuation of a move and is often near its halfway point.

GAP (Up). Occurs when today's lowest price minus yesterday's highest price exceeds zero.

GROWTH STOCK. A company that is expected to increase its earnings rapidly. It usually has a low dividend payout ratio and a high multiple of price-earnings ratio.

GTC. Good until canceled. When you place an order to buy or sell securities at a specific price, GTC means that the order will be left with the broker for execution until you cancel it.

HEDGE. The purchase and sale of securities likely to rise and fall in opposite directions under the same conditions. For example: The purchase of a common stock and sale of a warrant or a call option short. In hedging potential profits are sacrificed in order to reduce the level of risk.

HEDGE (Variable). An option strategy that involves writing one covered option and one or more uncovered options.

HORIZONTAL SPREAD. Same as Calendar Spread.

INSTITUTIONAL INVESTORS. Organizations managing large sums of financial assets. They include the following: banks, insurance companies, mutual funds, pension funds, and trusts. When buying or selling large blocks of securities, they have a significant effect on market prices and market liquidity. For example, Insurance Company A owns a large block of General Motors stock. One day it decides to sell this stock. In the absence of buyers, GM stock will probably drop sharply on that day.

IN-THE-MONEY OPTION (Call Option). An option whose exercise price is below the current market price of the underlying stock. For example, when the market price of a stock is 30 and the call option has a striking price of 20, the call option is in-the-money 10 points. If the option is exercised immediately this 10-point value can be realized.

INTRINSIC VALUE OF AN OPTION. It is the immediate exercise value of an option. Intrinsic value equals the market price of the stock minus the striking price of the option. For example, if the market price of a stock is 35 and the call option has a striking price of 30, the call option has an intrinsic value of 5 points, which can be realized if the option is exercised immediately. Conversely, with a stock at 25, a put at 30 has $5 intrinsic value. (See also In-the-Money.)

LEVERAGE. The use of securities as collateral against a loan to purchase additional securities — with the expectation that the earnings and growth of the securities will be greater than the interest cost. An increase in the price of the securities will result in a higher rate of return than could have been obtained by purchase of the securities with no borrowed funds.

LIQUIDITY. A market in a stock is considered liquid when it can absorb a large increase in volume with only a small change in price. A market in a stock is not liquid when it is difficult to absorb a large increase in volume unless a large change in the price of the stock takes place.

LONG POSITION. Possession of a stock or stock option, either fully paid or on margin.

MAJOR MARKET INDEX FUTURES (MMI). A broad-based stock index that measures the performance of 20 blue-chip stocks listed on the New York Stock Exchange. These issues represent well-known, established corporations, who are leaders in their respective industries. The MMI is a price-weighted index, calculated by summing the price of the individual stocks and dividing that sum by a divisor. This divisor changes from time to time to account for stock splits and stock dividends.

MARGIN TRANSACTION. Purchase of securities in which the purchaser puts up only part (a margin) of the total capital. The remainder is borrowed, using the purchases securities as collateral. Buying on margin creates more opportunities for a better rate of return, although the risks are greater. The amount of margin allowable is regulated by the Federal Reserve Board.

MATURITY DATE. When principal of debt must be paid.

MODEL (Decision Rules). A decision model is a set of tests. It states the relevant factors to the decision-maker. These factors are a set of questions which must be answered before the decision-maker arrives at a conclusion. The decision rules must be specific, qualified, and tested over a period of time. Such a test might involve the use of the computer. It is very difficult to test models manually since a test may involve many stocks and many years of data. A better model means better performance, although different users may require different sets of decision rules. If a model is unsatisfactory, a new one should be developed.

Models are developed as a result of practical historical observation: a theory is later developed to try to explain the observations.

MONETARY AGGREGATES (M_0, M_1, M_2 .....M_7). Monetary aggregates are various measures of the nation's stock of money. These statistics are released by the Federal Reserve Bank and indicate changes in levels of money supply and interest rates may go up, an unfavorable development for the stock market. When monetary aggregates go down, the Federal Reserve may not find it necessary to tighten money supply, a favorable development for the stock market. There are eight monetary aggregates, which are defined as follows: Higher subscripts indicate more inclusive aggregates.

M_0 = currency in the hands of the public

M_1 = M_0 + demand (checking) deposits at commerical banks

M_2 = M_1 + time deposits at commerical banks other than large negotiable certificates of deposit

M_3 = M_2 + mutual savings bank deposits, savings and loan association shares, and credit union shares

M_4 = M_2 + large negotiable certificates of deposit

M_5 = M_3 + large negotiable certificates of deposit

M_6 = M_5 + short-term marketable U.S. government securities

M_7 = M_6 + short-term commercial paper

MOVING AVERAGES. An average covering a specified period of time (usually days or weeks) and related to price or volume. The most commonly used moving averages are 200-day, 150-day, 30-day, 10-day, and

3-day. Moving averages enable the analyst to ignore shorter-term volatility, which might be due to random causes, and help determine the overall basic move or trend. It is a very important tool in trend analysis and is used in most time indicators. In a three-day moving average, for example, a three-day total is maintained by the addition of the data for the current day and subtraction of the data for the fourth previous day. One-third of the total is the moving average.

MUNICIPAL SECURITIES. Tax-exempt securities. The debt obligations of states and their political subdivisions. They are issued to raise money for public purposes such as water and sewer systems, highway construction, schools, housing, and hospitals.

MUNICIPAL SECURITIES TRUST. Unit trusts with fixed portfolios of tax-exempt bonds that are purchased with the intention of holding them to maturity. However, you as the individual investor can sell your interest in the trust at any time. They are similar to municipal bond mutual funds in terms of their tax-free income, but with a basic difference in that the portfolio of the unit trust is known when it is started and no new bonds can be added.

NAKED OPTION (Call). A call option written by a writer who does not own the underlying stock. Cash must remain in the writer's investment account to honor this contract if required.

NASD (National Association of Securities Dealers). Members of NASD are broker-dealers who have an office in the United States and who agree to follow the NASD's rules and regulations.

NONRANDOM CONDITION (Timing Indicators). Occurs when a timing indicator reaches an extreme level. Under this condition there is a high probability of accuracy in predicting a market change of trend.

ODD-LOT. Stock purchased or sold in lots of fewer than 100 shares. Buyers of odd lots are usually small investors.

OPEN INTEREST. Open interest on the options market is the number of shares represented by option contracts outstanding, at a particular time.

OPEN ORDER. Same as Good Till Canceled (GTC) order.

OPENING PURCHASE TRANSACTION. A transaction in which an investor intends to become the holder of an option.

OPENING SALE TRANSACTION. A transaction in which an investor intends to become the writer (or seller) of an option.

OPERATIONS RESEARCH (Definition). Operations Research is an approach to problem solving that involves the application of scientific tools, techniques, and methods. It may also involve some experimentation and often includes the use of the computer. Some of these techniques and scientific tools include: probability theory, critical path methods, corporate profits models, statistics, forecasting models, inventory models, queuing models, simulation models, computer applications and systems analysis, information systems analysis, trend analysis models, and exponential smoothing. One characteristic of these techniques is that they help solve a unique class of problems involving the interaction of components of systems and come up with a solution that will help accomplish the overall objectives of an organization.

OPERATIONS RESEARCH (Objectives). The objective of Operations Research is to help managers make better and more effective decisions regarding both old and new problems. Rather than looking for the best theoretical solution, this type of research helps achieve the most practical one under real existing circumstances. To achieve these pragmatic goals, the operations researcher will most often follow a procedure which includes: formulating the problem, constructing the mathematical model, deriving the solution from the model, testing the model, establishing operating controls, and implementation.

OPTION. Webster defines an option as "a stipulated privilege of buying and selling a stated property, service, or commodity at a given price within a specified time." An option is a contract allowing its holder to buy from an investor, or to sell to another investor, 100 shares of a stock at a specified price (exercise price) within a specified time (expiration date).

OPTIONS CLEARING CORPORATION. The issuer and guarantor of all listed option contracts. It is owned proportionately by each of the exchanges trading listed options contracts. Before engaging in the purchasing or writing of traded options, investors should read and understand the Options Clearing Corporation prospectus.

OPTION PRICES. The premium the buyer pays to acquire the option and which the writer receives for selling the option. Option prices will go up when more people are interested in buying and fewer people are interested in writing. Conversely, option prices will go down when more people are interested in writing and fewer people are interested in buying.

OPTION WRITER (Seller). See Writer.

OUT-OF-THE-MONEY. An option in which exercise price is above the current market price of the stock. For example, when the market price of a stock is 30, and the call option has a striking price of 40, the call option is out of the money 10 points. If the option is exercised immediately, a loss of 10 points will be realized.

OVERBOUGHT. When an upside move in the price of a stock (or the market) has extended too far or too fast, possibly above the trend channel, and a correction is expected. Selling into an overbought condition will generate nonrandom returns.

OVERSOLD. When a downside move in the price of a stock (or the market) has extended too far or too fast, possibly below the trend channel, and a correction is expected. Buying into an oversold condition will generate nonrandom returns.

PENETRATION. Occurs when a stock breaks through a resistance level by a minimum percentage (a commonly used minimum is 4 percent); the old resistance level then becomes the new support level. Conversely, when a stock goes down below a support level by a minimum percentage, the old support level becomes the new resistance level.

POINT AND FIGURE. A method of recording price activity which disregards time intervals or volume. Only trends or changes in price trends are relevant.

POINT AND FIGURE CHARTS. Point and Figure Charts are used by many investors to (1) keep stocks under constant supervision, (2) spot buy formations, (3) watch for sell signals and short sale opportunities, (4) formulate price objectives, (5) be warned of resistance areas, (6) foresee support areas, and (7) possess a visual price history. (See Chart — Chapter 5, Page 97).

PORTFOLIO. Groups of securities including common and preferred stocks, bonds, notes, cash, convertible securities, or options combined in a stated amount or percentage to meet defined investment objectives.

PRICE OBJECTIVE. A potential price of a stock when it reaches the next support or resistance level. Could apply to short, intermediate, or long-term trends.

PRICE PER EARNINGS RATIO. Is calculated by dividing the market price of the stock by the earnings per share. For example, if the common stock is selling at $40 a share, and the earnings per share for the current year is $4 a share, the current PE ratio is 10.

PRIME RATE. The interest rate charged by banks to their best customers on short-term loans.

PROBABILITY. The probability of an outcome is the percentage of times the outcome will occur if the event is repeated a great many times. Probability theory deals with random events and is a practical measure of uncertainty. High probability is a state which is likely to happen. Low probability is a state which is unlikely to happen. Under certain conditions there is always a chance that the decision-maker may be wrong. (See also Random Moves.)

PUT OPTION. An option to sell.

QUANTITATIVE ANALYSIS. Based on facts and figures, rather than on judgement and opinion.

RALLY. Technical uptrend in market prices.

RANDOM MOVES OF STOCK PRICES. Many academicians claim that the stock market is totally random. The scientific usage of the word random is not much different from its everyday usage: a random variable is a value or magnitude that can change, occurrence after occurrence, event after event, in no predictable sequence. We can say that a sample is random if every element has an equal chance of being selected from the sample. Randomness is generally interpreted as lack of bias — where no one item is preferred. Under the random theory of the market, the probability of making an incorrect decision is the same as the probability of making a correct one. Under certain market conditions, moves can be predicted with high probability, resulting in better-than-average return on investment. Random moves are nonexplanatory moves. We cannot explain why certain moves take place at a specific time in a specific direction.

NONRANDOM CONTROL LIMITS (Timing Indicators). The concept of nonrandom control limits specifies that when a timing indicator level is within certain limits the investment results obtained by using the indicator are random. But when the indicator's level exceeds these limits (upper or lower) nonrandom results will be achieved. For example, historical analysis will show that when the trading index is between the limits of .70 and 1.40, results are random; when the index is below .70 and above 1.40, results are nonrandom. Within the limits, investment results will not be better than average and therefore trader activity should be minimized. Beyond the control limits, results are of a nonrandom nature and should yield better-than-average return on investment.

RANDOM VARIABLE. A value or magnitude that can change in no predictable sequence, occurrence after occurrence, event after event.

RANDOM WALK THEORY. The theory that market moves are random and unpredictable; i.e., that the cycles or trends of stock prices are as true as the chart patterns derived from random tosses of the coin or a gambler's runs of good and bad luck.

RATE OF RETURN ON INVESTMENT. A measure of the income and capital gain generated by an investment relative to the amount invested.

RATIO WRITING. When several calls are sold against each 100 shares of the underlying stock. A ratio of 2 for 1 indicates that 2 calls were sold against a position of 100 shares.

REFLEX REACTION. A short-term move in the opposite direction of a major trend which corrects an overbought or oversold condition.

REGULAR WAY TRANSACTION. Settlement of trade (purchase or sale) due on the fifth business day following the stock trade date. In the case of a purchase, you must pay on or before the settlement date. In the case of a sale, you will receive payment on or before the settlement date.

REGULATION T. A Federal Reserve rule that limits the amount of credit that a broker-dealer may extend to a customer.

RELATIVE STRENGTH. The ratio of a stock price to a chosen market index over a specified time period.

RELATIVE STRENGTH LINE. The line that connects the points of the relative strength ratios. A rising line means that the stock is relatively stronger than the market index; a declining line indicates that the stock is relatively weaker than the market index.

RESISTANCE LEVEL. A price (or a price range) at which a price advance is expected to stop (or reverse) due to increase in selling activity. It represents concentration of supply. Effective use of resistance levels is an important timing tool to options writers.

RETURN ON INVESTMENT. Return is composed of two elements: (1) appreciation or capital gain in a security and (2) the yield in dividends or interest of a security. Net return is the same figure modified by appropriate tax adjustments.

REVERSE OPTION HEDGE. Ownership of more than one call option for each round lot of an underlying stock in which the owner is short. This position is taken in very volatile stocks where violent rapid moves in either direction are expected.

RISK-INVESTMENTS. The degree of uncertainty in appreciation and/or income of a security over future time periods. When the level of risks rises, the possibility of an investment loss increases.

RISK/REWARD RATIO. A measure of possible loss versus potential gain under a particular investment strategy. Also refers to the position of the closing price in relation to the next support and resistance levels. The owner is short. This position is taken in very volatile stocks where violent, rapid moves in either direction are expected.

ROUND LOT. A lot of 100 shares. Stocks traded on listed exchanges in 100-share lots.

SECONDARY MARKET (Option). A provision within exchange markets for liquidating transactions (for example, the provision by which option writers can "buy back" their options). This secondary market enables investors to buy and sell options in the same way they buy and sell securities on the N.Y.S.E. or the A.S.E. It should be noted that exchange-traded options differ from over-the-counter options in that an adjustment is made for ordinary cash dividends.

SECONDARY OFFERINGS. Planned stock distributions, usually by insiders or majority stockholders. They frequently occur at the end of a bull market and near major market tops. Sellers take advantage of high prices and usually sell the stock to the over-optimistic public. Secondary offering activity is very low in bear markets.

SECURITIES ANALYSIS. The evaluation of financial statements and results of operations of a corporation.

SELLING AGAINST THE BOX. See Against the Box.

SENTIMENT INDICATORS. Market indicators that try to gauge changes in investor psychology underlying investment decisions.

SERIES OF OPTIONS. Options of the same class, having same exercise price and expiration time.

SHORT AGAINST THE BOX. (See Against the Box).

SHORT INTEREST. Represents the total number of shares that have been sold and remain in a short position as of a specific date. This information is published in the financial papers on the 20th of each month, as of the 15th of the month. The total number of shares which are short in a specific stock are given in comparison to their short interest of the previous month. Only stocks which have a short interest over 5,000 shares or more are listed.

SHORT SALE. Sale of a stock the investor does not own in anticipation of a decline in price. When the price has declined, the stock is then purchased to cover the (short) sale. This process involves a high degree of risk, as the stock sold was borrowed by the seller and must be bought back, if the lender so requests. Short selling attracts speculators, as profits are often made much faster on the downside.

SHORT SQUEEZE. A short squeeze occurs when traders who sold borrowed shares, in anticipation of replacing them at lower prices, are forced to "cover" those borrowed shares by buying shares, even at higher prices. When a wave of short covering takes place, prices tend to jump because of the increased demand for the "short" shares.

SIDEWAY MARKET. Price fluctuations within a neutral trend.

SPECIALIST. A member of the stock exchange who, acting as a broker for other members, keeps a record of and executes selling and buying orders only of specified stocks. It would be impossible for each member to carry out all the orders of his firm. A specialist is also a member who specializes in making a market, which results in narrowing the price spread between bid and offer, in one or more stocks. He subordinates his personal position to orders from other brokers or his own customers. His responsibility is to maintain an orderly market, with a narrow spread between bid and ask prices; this may require risking his own capital.

SPECULATOR. A buyer or seller of securities who expects to make a large profit if successful, but may experience a large loss if unsuccessful.

SPLIT. See *Stock Split*.

SPREAD (Horizontal). A horizontal spread occurs when two options with the same underlying stock have different expiration dates but the same striking price.

SPREAD (Vertical). A vertical spread occurs when two options with the same underlying stock have different exercise prices but the same expiration date.

STABILIZATION. A period of sideway price action, usually before a trend is reversed. Sometimes called basing or accumulation after a decline and top formation or distribution after an advance.

STOCK DIVIDEND. A dividend payable in stock rather than cash. It is a distribution of additional shares to existing stockholders. Although each stockholder receives additional shares, the total number of shares outstanding also increases. As a result, the investor's proportionate ownership in the corporation does not change. A stock dividend is a nontaxable transaction.

STOCK SPLIT. A stock is split when the company divides its shares. If a corporation has 5 million shares outstanding, and splits them two for one, the new number of shares outstanding is 10 million. Therefore, if you own 100 shares of the ABC Company before the split, you will own 200 shares after the split. The split does not change the company's capital stock or its paid-in surplus accounts. The split divides the market price in proportion to the split ratio. In a two for one split, the market price of the stock is divided by two. A $70 per share stock will sell at $35 after the split. Although a stock split will reduce a high-priced stock to a more popular price range, the split in itself does not make any profits for you as a shareholder.

STOP LOSS ORDERS. An order given by an investor to a broker, in advance, to sell a stock if its price declines below a certain point. It is used to limit the extent of potential losses. Loss limits are also established to stop losing earned gains. Premature exit, however, can push you out of a position that later may become profitable.

STRADDLE. A combination of both a put and a call option on the same stock, at the same striking price, for the same period of time, and for which the seller receives a single premium. The buyer can exercise one or both options on or before the expiration date.

STRAP. A combination option consisting of two calls and one put.

STRATEGY. Detailed planning of the movements or steps to be taken prior to making a final investment decision. Also skilled management in choosing the best alternatives for attaining predetermined investment goals.

STRIKING PRICE (Exercise Price). The price at which an option holder can buy 100 shares of the underlying stock in the case of a call, or sell them in the case of a put. On option exchanges the exercise price is set in advance and does not change during the life of the option. However, additional exercise prices may be introduced when the underlying stock's price changes substantially in order that the exercise price remains close to the price of the underlying stock. New striking prices are normally introduced at 5-point intervals for stocks trading below 50; at 10-point intervals for stocks trading between 50 and 100; and at 20-point intervals for stocks trading above 100.

STRIP. A combination option consisting of one call and two puts.

SUPPORT LEVEL. A price or price range at which the price decline is expected to stop or reverse due to an increase in buying activity. It represents concentration of demand. A support level may also exist at a price at which a large number of shares has changed hands in the past. Effective use of support levels is an important timing tool to options buyers. Usually three levels of support and resistance are used: short, intermediate, and long term.

SWAP. The sale of a security and substitution of it by the purchase of another security. Reasons for a swap could be, for example, to reduce or defer taxes, to increase current yield, to shorten maturities, or to upgrade the quality of a portfolio.

TAX SELLING. Sale of a stock to record a loss for tax purposes. Tax selling often occurs at year end. Some investors take advantage of price declines and shop for bargains.

TAX SHELTER. An investment whose primary purpose is to reduce your current tax payment. It can be achieved either by eliminating a tax payment, or by deferring the payment into future years. The most popular tax shelters are retirement plans such as IRA and Keogh. Real estate investment is also a popular tax shelter because of the depreciation deductions.

TAX SWAP. Timely maneuvers during the year that can help you to gain a tax-favored position. Prudent use of swapping may help you consolidate portions of your portfolio, possibly increase current income, or lessen taxes without losing current income.

TECHNICIAN. The technician studies the historical price and volume patterns of a stock or of the market as a whole. The securities analyst studies the fundamentals of the operating company.

TECHNICAL ANALYSIS. The study of factors affecting the supply and demand of stocks. These factors include price and volume movement as well as daily, weekly, and monthly market averages. Technical analysis assumes that the price at which a stock is sold or bought is determined by the level of expectation of all investors and traders, both the sophisticated institution and the unsophisticated public. There is a distinction between knowing the company fundamentally and knowing the stock technically. The experienced technical analyst concentrates on extremes created by changes in investor psychology. He also concentrates on an analysis of money flow. Often technical analysis is thought of simply as chart reading. In fact, this represents only a small segment of the art.

TECHNICAL RALLY. Occurs when prices move up after a rather sharp decline. This rally is a reaction to the sharp decline and will not be sustained.

TENDER OFFER. An announcement of a bid to acquire some or all of the securities of a corporation. It is often used in a takeover of one company by another.

TERM (Intermediate). A period of less than six months (and usually more than three months).

TERM (Long). A period exceeding six months (minimum holding period for capital gain tax) and sometimes one complete Bear-Bull cycle.

TERM (Short). A period of less than three months but more than one month.

THIRD MARKET. Buying and selling of exchange-listed securities by over-the-counter dealers. Third-market transactions are reported on the exchanges' consolidated tape.

TRADING INDEX (TRIN). The ratio of the advance/decline issues ratio to the upside-downside volume ratio. It compares the number of advancing and declining issues to the volume of advancing and declining issues. A reading of 0.75 or lower for a 10-day average indicates an overbought market. A reading of 1.25 or higher for a 10-day average indicates an oversold market.

TREASURY BILL. Short-term U.S. obligations, maturing in less than a year. They do not pay interest, but instead are sold at a discount from face value.

TREND CALCULATIONS. A trend can be defined as the difference between two averages within a specific time period. It represents the direction of a moving average. For example, if the average price last week was 19, and the average price this week is 20, the trend is equal to 1.

TREND CHANNEL. The area between two parallel trend lines. The channel contains almost all price movements within a specific time period.

TRENDLESS MARKET. A neutral market. Prices fluctuate at random without any sustained up or down moves.

TREND LINE. A line that connects two or more points on a chart and represents the up or down slope of a movement over a specific period of time. Stock prices tend to move in trends until the supply/demand relationship changes. An increase in supply will cause a downtrend and an increase in demand will cause an uptrend.

TREND (Primary). A movement up, down, or neutral that lasts for more than one year.

TREND (Secondary). A short-term or intermediate correction that takes place within a trend channel; i.e., a short-term down movement within a primary uptrend, or a short-term uptrend within a primary downtrend.

TRIN. See Trading Index.

UNCOVERED WRITER. A writer of an option who is not a covered writer. An uncovered call is a naked call. You do not own the underlying stock.

UNDERLYING STOCK. A stock purchased by an investor for which an option has been bought or sold, a security subject to being purchased upon the exercise of an option.

UNDERWRITER. An investment banker who purchases securities from the issuer and resells it to the public.

UNIFORM GIFT TO MINOR ACT. A law relating to gifts to minors. When an account is opened with a broker, only one adult can serve as a custodian.

UNIT TRUSTS. An investment company that assembles a fixed portfolio of securities and then offers interest (units) in that trust to investors.

UPTICK. A transaction is said to occur on an uptick when it takes place at a price higher than the previous transaction.

UPTICK-DOWNTICK BLOCK RATIO. The number of NYSE blocks (minus opening blocks) which traded on upticks as a percent of the number of NYSE blocks traded on downticks.

UPTICK (Zero). A transaction which occurs at the same price as the previous transaction, but higher than the last different price. A zero downtick is a transaction which occurs at the same price as the previous transaction, but lower than the last different price.

UPTREND. Refers to an upward movement of a series of data over a specific period of time.

VARIABLE HEDGE. A strategy which involves writing one covered option and one or more uncovered options for the purpose of achieving a greater downside price protection.

VOLATILITY. The degree of stock price fluctuation over a specific period of time (usually a day, week, or month) measured as a percent change of price movement. The degree of annual price fluctuation of the stock often has a much larger range than the annual fluctuation in balance sheet values or earnings figures of the company itself. The volatility of the underlying stock is an important factor influencing the price of options.

VOLUME (Definition). Total trading activity in a security, a group of securities, or the whole market for a specific period of time, usually a day, week, or month.

VOLUME, ON BALANCE (OBV). A cumulative volume figure over a specific period of time, which depends on the direction of the price movement. For example, when the change in price is positive the cumulative volume figure for that period will increase; when the change in price is negative the cumulative volume figure will decrease. OBV is used as an indicator of the amount of money going in and out of a stock. On balance volume is equal to the previous on balance volume plus or minus the current daily volume. The (+) or (-) will depend on the direction of the price from the previous day. An increase in OBV indicates that the stock is under accumulation. A decline in OBV indicates that the stock is under distribution.

VOLUME (Tick). Similar to on-balance except that the base is not a time period but an individual transaction. For example, for any one day in a particular stock, the net tick volume is computed by subtracting the total volume which occurred on downticks from the total volume which occurred on upticks.

WARRANTS. A warrant gives its owner the right to buy common stock. The warrant agreement specifies the terms of this right, including a specified exercise price and a specific expiration date. Warrants are often issued by corporations in conjunction with the sale of common stock or bonds and usually have a lifespan of several years. They offer the investor, through leverage, a greater potential return on investment than the common stock that the warant option entitles the investor to buy. A stock warrant often has a longer life than a stock option. Warrants usually are exercisable on a one-for-one basis (one warrant for one common share). Options usually are exercisable on a one-for-100 basis (one warrant for 100 shares).

WHIPSAW. Occurs when an indicator gives an incorrect bullish or bearish signal for several days and then reverses itself, resulting in losses to investors. It can also occur when an alert model gives a signal to buy or sell (by being oversensitive) when no signal should have been given.

WRITER (Option). The person who writes the option; i.e., the person who sells or creates the option.

YIELD (Current). The current annual income from a security as a percentage if its current cost. For example, when you receive an annual interest income of $75.00 from a bond that is selling at $950.00, the current yield is calculated by dividing 75 by 950. It is equal to 0.0789, or 7.89%.

YIELD TO MATURITY. The average annual return on an investment based on the interest rate, price, face value, redemption value, number of interest periods per year, and the time left to maturity. Some of the difference between yield to maturity and current yield is that the former takes into consideration the capital gain appreciation to par of a bond bought at a discount and capital loss to par of a bond bought at a premium.

ZERO COUPON OBLIGATIONS. Notes and bonds purchased at a discount from par. You do not receive any coupon interest monthly, semiannually, or annually, as in the case of a regualr bond. You receive a single payment at maturity. The yield to maturity is guaranteed and is based on the discount at the time of purchase.

Bibliography and Suggested Readings

ARBITRAGE

Boesky, Ivan F., *Merger Mania* (New York: Holt, Rinehart, Winston, 1985).

ECONOMICS

Galbraith, John K., *The Great Crash 1929* (Boston: Houghton Mifflin Company, 1961).

Heilbroner, Robert L., and Lester C. Thurow, *The Economic Problem*, seventh edition (Englewood Cliffs, NJ: Prentice-Hall, Inc. 1984).

FUNDAMENTAL ANALYSIS

Bernstein, Leopold A., *Understanding Corporate Reports: A Guide to Financial Statement Analysis* (Homewood, IL: Dow Jones-Irwin, Inc., 1975).

Graham, Benjamin, David L. Dodd, and Sidney Cottle, with Charles Tatham, *Security Analysis*, fourth edition (New York: McGraw-Hill, 1962).

GLOSSARY

Pessin, Allan H. and Joseph A. Ross, *Words of Wall Street: 2000 Investment Terms Defined* (Homewood, IL: Dow Jones-Irwin, 1983).

INVESTMENT ANALYSIS (GENERAL)

Bellemore, Douglas H., Herbert E. Phillips, and John C. Ritchie, *Investment Analysis and Portfolio Selection: An Integrated Approach* (Cincinnati, OH: South-Western Publishing Co., 1979).

Thorp, Edward O. and Sheen T. Kassouf, *Beat the Market* (New York: Random House, 1967).

INVESTMENT PHILOSOPHY

Baruch, Bernard M., *My Own Story* (New York: Henry Holt & Company, 1957).

Getty, Paul J., *How to Be Rich* (Chicago: Playboy Press, 1961).

Loeb, Gerald M., *The Battle for Investment Survival* (New York: Simon & Schuster, 1965).

Mackay Charles, LL.D, *Extraordinary Popular Delusions and the Madness of Crowds* (U.S.A.: L.C. Page & Co., seventeenth printing, 1969).

Martin, Ralph G., *The Wizard of Wall Street* (New York: William Morrow and Co., 1965).

MUTUAL FUNDS

Investor's Directory, Your Guide to Mutual Funds 1985-1986, published by the No-Load Mutual Fund Association, Inc., 11 Penn Plaza, Suite 2204, New York, NY 10001.

1985 Mutual Fund Fact Book, by the Investment Company Institute, Washington, D.C.

OPTIONS STRATEGIES

Gastineau, Gary L., *The Stock Options Manual*, second edition. (New York: McGraw-Hill Book Company, 1978).

Saint-Peter, Norman, *How to Make Money in Stock Options* (Englewood Cliffs, NJ: Prentice-Hall, Inc., 1984).

Understanding the Risks and Uses of Listed Options. Booklet prepared jointly by the American Stock Exchange, Inc., the Chicago Board Options Exchange, the New York Stock Exchange, Inc., the

Pacific Stock Exchange, Inc., the Philadelphia Stock Exchange, Inc., and The Options Clearing Corporation, September 1983.

Characteristics and Risks of Standardized Options. Booklet prepared jointly by the American Stock Exchange, Inc., Chicago Board Options Exchange, National Association of Securities Dealers, Inc., New York Stock Exchange, Inc., Pacific Stock Exchange, Inc., Philadelphia Stock Exchange, Inc., and The Options Clearing Corporation, September 1985.

PERSONAL FINANCIAL PLANNING

Scott, Carole Elizabeth. *Your Financial Plan: A Cosumer's Guide* (New York: Harper & Row, Publishers, Inc., 1979).

PORTFOLIO MANAGEMENT

Cohen, Jerome B., Zinbarg, Edward D., and Zeikel, Arthur. *Investment Analysis and Portfolio Management, Third Edition* (Homewood, IL: Richard D. Irwin, Inc., 1977).

TAXES

Explanation of Tax Reform Act of 1984, (Chicago: Commerce Clearing House, Inc., 1984).

Tax Considerations in Using CBOE Option, (Chicago Board Options Exchange, LaSalle at Van Buren, Chicago, IL 60605, 1984).

TECHNICAL ANALYSIS

Edwards, Robert D. and John Magee, *Technical Analysis of Stock Trends,* thirteenth printing (Springfield, MA: John Magee, 1962).

Fosbac, Norman G., *Stock Market Logic: A Sophisticated Approach to Profits on Wall Street* (Ft. Lauderdale, FL: The Institute for Econometric Research, 1976, 1984).

Frost, A.J., and Prechter, Robert J., *Elliot Wave Principle* (New York: New Classic Library, Inc., 1978, 1985).

Granville, Joseph E., *Granville's New Strategy of Daily Stock Market Timing for Maximum Profit* (Englewood Cliffs, NJ: Prentice-Hall, Inc. 1976).

Jiler, William L., *How Charts Can Help You in the Stock Market* (New York: Trendline — A division of Standard & Poors Corporation, ninth printing, 1970).

Merrill, Arthur A., *Behavior of Prices on Wall Street, Second Edition*, (Chappaqua, NY: Analysis Press, 1984).

Sources
of Investment Data

CORPORATE REPORTS

> The annual report
> Quarterly and other interim reports
> Securities and Exchange Commission filings —
>> Report Form 10-K
> Statements by corporate spokesmen

FINANCIAL REPORTING SERVICES

> Moody's Investment Service
> Standard & Poors
> Value Line

BROKERAGE REPORTS

> Research reports
> Prospectuses

FEDERAL RESERVE PUBLICATIONS

> *U.S. Financial Data*, The Federal Reserve Bank
> of St. Louis, P.O. Box 442, St. Louis, Missouri 63166.

PERIODICALS CONTAINING
BUSINESS INFORMATION
Newsweek
Business Week
Fortune
Forbes

FINANCIAL NEWS
(INCLUDING PRICE QUOTATIONS)
Barron's
The Wall Street Journal
The New York Times

INDEX

205

Index